KT-223-502

PENGUIN BOOKS
You Are What You Eat Cookbook

Dr Gillian McKeith (PhD) is an internationally acclaimed
holistic nutritionist. She is the presenter of *You Are What
You Eat*, the hit Celador primetime television programme for
Channel 4. She is also the author of the bestselling *You Are
What You Eat*, *Dr Gillian McKeith's Ultimate Health Plan* and
Living Food for Health (Piatkus). Raised in Scotland, Gillian
now travels extensively, giving lectures and seminars.

Over 150 healthy and delicious recipes

Dr Gillian McKeith's
you are what you eat
Cookbook

A Celador Production as seen on Channel Four
www.youarewhatyoueat.tv

PENGUIN BOOKS

PENGUIN BOOKS

Published by the Penguin Group

Penguin Books Ltd, 80 Strand, London WC2R 0RL, England

Penguin Group (USA) Inc., 375 Hudson Street, New York, New York 10014, USA

Penguin Group (Canada), 90 Eglinton Avenue East, Suite 700,
Toronto, Ontario, Canada M4P 2Y3 (a division of Pearson Penguin Canada Inc.)

Penguin Ireland, 25 St Stephen's Green, Dublin 2, Ireland
(a division of Penguin Books Ltd)

Penguin Group (Australia), 250 Camberwell Road, Camberwell,
Victoria 3124, Australia (a division of Pearson Australia Group Pty Ltd)

Penguin Books India Pvt Ltd, 11 Community Centre,
Panchsheel Park, New Delhi – 110 017, India

Penguin Group (NZ), 67 Apollo Drive, Mairangi Bay, Auckland 1310,
New Zealand (a division of Pearson New Zealand Ltd)

Penguin Books (South Africa) (Pty) Ltd, 24 Sturdee Avenue,
Rosebank, Johannesburg 2196, South Africa

Penguin Books Ltd, Registered Offices: 80 Strand, London WC2R 0RL, England

www.penguin.com

First published 2005
Published in paperback 2007

1

Set in Trade Gothic and New Clarendon
Designed and typeset by Smith & Gilmour, London
Printed in England by Clays Ltd, St Ives plc

ISBN: 978-0-141-02976-4

CONTENTS

INTRODUCTION
MY STORY

I truly believe anyone can be a great cook as long as they have the will to do it. When I was a wee lass at Perth High School I remember making cheese flan in Home Economics. The funny thing was, I hadn't even tasted the flan because at the time I detested the idea of eating cheese. But somehow I had been so passionate about my recipe that my cookery teacher gave me top marks, because my heart and mind had been in the right place.

My younger brother David had different views about my culinary skills, and when we were growing up he spent the entire time complaining to Mum and Dad that I couldn't even toast bread properly. OK, it's true that for some reason my toast always came out pitch-black like coal . . . Anyway, David always used to say that I'd burn the house down one day – a statement I took to be completely ludicrous . . . until that fateful rainy day when I was 17 and had just received my letter of acceptance into Edinburgh University. I was feeling really excited and preoccupied – and, of course, the bread was toasting away in the toaster – when, all of a sudden, the smell of burning wheat seemed to be permeating my bedroom.

I quickly darted into the kitchen, to be greeted by what looked like a scene from *The Towering Inferno*. My toast had caught fire and the flames had spread to the counter tops and walls. I was terrified – not just at the thought of burning down our family home, but at what my dad would say. Then, right on cue, David burst on the scene and quickly and efficiently proceeded to extinguish the fire with buckets of water and heavy wet towels.

So I am no Michelin-star chef – I am just a mother who wants the best for her family, and a holistic nutritionist who wants the best health and purest food for you. I just happen to have developed lots of healthy, fun and easy recipes over the years as part of my job. My recipes are quick to prepare – many only take a few minutes – and they're dead simple. If I can make them, anyone can!

Writing these recipes for you and making them readily available was something that was very important to me, because I understand first-hand how essential support like this can be to achieve wellness and a fit body. When I was twenty-something, I lived in Spain and survived on a diet of Spanish éclairs, paella, chocolate and sangrias. When

I got back to Britain I was chubby, had spots all over my face and felt constantly tired, listless and demotivated. A special diet could be my answer, I thought. A simple food plan. So for eight weeks I ate almost nothing but pork luncheon meats – or, to be precise, three slices of thin ham on two pieces of white bread. And I ate that for breakfast, lunch and dinner every day. As you can imagine, I felt and looked terrible. Over time, my unhealthy eating habits continued to play havoc with my body, energy levels and general wellbeing. It was this degeneration in my health that was the key motivating factor in my embarking on a new healthy lifestyle, and a diet of living foods.

When I finally turned my life and health around through natural nutrition and good food, I realized that (a) healthy recipes can be easy to prepare; (b) healthy meals can be quick, exciting and fun; (c) you can make food taste great even without any experience or training; and (d) healthy food can make you feel and look well, because *you really are what you eat.* All you need is the desire and the will to feel and be well.

The recipes in this book are easy, colourful and utterly delicious, and I really hope you love them as much as I do. But they're really just the beginning. Once you've got to grips with them, I'd like you to feel empowered to experiment, using them as a basis for creating other tasty dishes of your own. All my recipes have the ability to enhance your health and wellbeing for a far happier, healthier, energized, fitter and sexier you. And best of all, they won't ever make you fat, which means you can eat as much as you like with them. So it's time to get cooking to your heart's (and tummy's) content.

Wishing you Love and Light, *Jillian*

ONE FOOD PHILOSOPHY

My food philosophy consists of a few simple guidelines. These are covered in much more detail in the book *You Are What You Eat*. Follow them and you'll be happier, healthier, fitter, stronger, sexier – and, oh yes, slimmer too, if that's what your body needs. Please understand that my philosophy isn't primarily about losing weight, but about being interested in eating good food and feeling really well. Just follow my plan and your body weight will regulate itself naturally. Believe me, I'm speaking from experience here. Now for those guides . . .

GUIDE NUMBER ONE:
Eat as much food as you want until you are satisfied, as long as you eat the right foods prepared in the right way

The right foods are the simplest foods that grow from the earth in their most unadulterated, organic form – fresh vegetables, seasonal fruits, sprouted seeds, raw nuts and seeds, grains, beans, legumes, pulses – and certain vegetable proteins such as tofu together with some fish or organic turkey or chicken. It's what I call the 'Diet of Abundance' – you'll find there are dozens of perfect foods you can eat all day long and feel great!

The recipes in this book will give you all the information you need on preparing these foods in the best way for optimum nutrition.

GUIDE NUMBER TWO:
Never get fixated on weight

If there's one thing I can teach you, it's that what you resist will persist. So if you become fixated on your weight, then you'll only make it a bigger issue for yourself. Ditch the weight issue. Forget it. It simply does not work. We've got more important things to do. Once you finally let the weight issue go, and adopt a new lifestyle plan, your body weight will regulate itself. Believe me, this is true.

In all my years in practice, I have never had to weigh a single client. Imagine that – a nutritionist consulting overweight clients who has no scales and doesn't ever weigh anyone. So don't forget: *you will get amazing results if you stop focusing on your weight and start focusing on eating the right foods.* Which brings me to . . .

GUIDE NUMBER THREE:
Don't do fad diets – they don't work in the long term

I've never seen a fad diet that really works in the long term. Some may work in the short term but all too often, once the dieter goes off their diet, they put the weight back on to an even greater extent than before. There's no end to the number and variations of these fad diets, and the problem I have with most of them is that they restrict too many different foods and food groups, leaving you nutritionally starved. Apart from anything else, some of them can cause a loss of essential fatty acids (EFAs) – which are actually needed for weight loss or weight management – mineral imbalances, vitamin deficiencies, gastric disturbances and hormonal problems. My recipes, on the other hand, will help you get stronger and better nourished because I won't be cutting out what your body needs. And, as you now know, when you care about good health first, the weight issue will fall into place.

GUIDE NUMBER FOUR:
This is a plan for life

This simple philosophy needs to become second nature. To start with, you might want to carry this book into the supermarket or health food store to make the right purchasing choices; use this book in the kitchen at home for recipes; take it to work for referring to quick snacks; take it to restaurants for meal ideas. The *You Are What You Eat* concepts integrate and inter-connect into every realm of your life. This is your route to wellness, happiness and a great body.

GUIDE NUMBER FIVE:

It's got to be my way or the highway

Human health doesn't respond fully enough to half measures so I want you to really go for it. It's not that I am some kind of perfectionist gone awry; I just want to make sure you have the best shot at feeling great. I know what shoddy health and excess weight feels like. I've been there. We've all been there. I know we can do far better together if you do what I tell you.

I remember a woman who came into my office for the first time. She was recovering from a very serious illness and wanted help with her nutrition.

I wanted so much for her to get well and felt that I could help her, but knew she would have to want it as much as me. As she walked in I greeted her with a warm smile. So far so good. Then she landed a large bottle of vodka on my desk with the immortal words, 'I'll do your diet, Darling, but I'm not giving up my vodka.'

There was a deafening silence, then I walked to the door and opened it, saying, 'You can leave now!'

She sat there, looking stunned, then blurted out, 'Do you know who I am? My husband is world famous. We are very wealthy people.'

So I gave her what-for: 'Go back to your husband with your bottle of poison and drain him, but you're not going to drain me. I don't care who you are, who your husband is, what you do or how much money you all have. It makes no difference to me. When it comes to health, we are one and the same. You are to leave now!'

I'd touched a nerve. She broke down into uncontrollable tears, sobbing bitterly, 'I am desperate. Please help me. I'll do anything you say.'

'Right,' I said. 'Take that bottle of alcohol and pour it down my office sink drain right now, and then we can get started.'

And she did. And we got started. And she never looked back. She consulted with me for years. She became a new woman with a new body and with new heights of energy, hopes and dreams.

For the next three months, I want you to eat according to my plan and recipes. After this first three-month period, you are welcome to introduce an 80:20 approach: do what I tell you 80 per cent of the time and you can be naughty 20 per cent of the time. So you see, things aren't so bad after all. But when you adopt my new ways, you may find that you enjoy the delicious taste of these healthy foods so much, and savour the feeling of wellness you have that you may not want to look back.

GUIDE NUMBER SIX:
Be creative and passionate in your cooking

What I want is to empower you to help yourself make the changes you need. This book will provide you with lots of ideas which I hope will not only keep you on the path to good health but also inspire you to create your own recipes.

Here's how it works. If you can make Hearty Lentil Stew (p.163), then you can make any stew. For example, you can change the lentils to kidney beans and the meal becomes a kidney bean stew. Change the kidney beans to chickpeas and it becomes a chickpea stew. Change the veggies, the herbs and seasonings that go with the beans and voilà – you have a whole new set of food creations that you have developed yourself. This is empowerment.

GUIDE NUMBER SEVEN:
Embrace change

We can often be our own worst enemies when it comes to change: 'I can't do this, I can't do that.' We too often give ourselves continuous negative messages with constant restrictive limits. Here are just some of the things my TV participants have thrown at me:

'I don't like beans.' (Before ever tasting them.)

'I hate the smell of brown rice.'

'Millet looks gross.'

The things we say to ourselves are listened to by our body at large. To involve yourself in my programme, you will need to be open to new ideas, new foods, new ways. So don't get stuck in the mud. This is where you take responsibility for yourself. Get unstuck and get moving and you will be truly free to pursue your dreams, hopes and goals for a deep, fulfilling life.

GUIDE NUMBER EIGHT:
Be in touch with your emotions

After many years of working in the field of nutritional health, juggling work, family life and everything else in between, I know from experience that it can be easy to lose yourself.

I once had a client who was in her late forties and grossly overweight. She showed me photographs of herself taken nearly 25 years earlier, in which she looked wonderful: not only slim but sparkly-eyed and literally lit up with energy. I asked her what had happened and she explained that for over 20 years she had been eating junk food for comfort.

Tears welled up in her eyes and, after gentle prompting, she slowly began to tell me how she had lost her baby daughter at just 22 days old. This woman had never been given counselling and had simply been using bad food to bury her pain for all that time. And it was only by opening up about her relationship with food that she had reached her most inner emotions, and realized how interconnected they had become.

I believe that our body, our emotions and what we eat are all intricately linked. Each affects the other. This woman's experience may be rather more pronounced than the norm, but there is a general lesson for everyone here. In order to become a balanced, harmonious and contented individual, and for your body to get the very best out of healthy food, you need to be in touch with yourself. Accept who you are. This is an important step towards being and staying healthy.

FOOD COMBINING MADE SIMPLE

The majority of the recipes in this book follow simple food combining rules. If you follow these guidelines you may lose weight if you need to, and will do it simply and healthily. Plus you'll say goodbye to gas, bloating and most digestive problems – and feel a million times better. However, once you have your weight and other diet-related issues resolved then you won't need to be quite so strict. It's still best to follow my guidelines as much as you can, though, as it's a sure path to feeling fantastic.

A more detailed explanation of food combining is in my previous book *You Are What You Eat*, but in very simple terms this is what you need to know:

GROUP 1: Proteins

» Cheese
» Eggs
» Fish
» Game/rabbit
» Meat
» Milk

» Nuts
» Poultry
» Shellfish
» Soybeans, tofu and soya products
» Yogurt

GROUP 2: Carbohydrates

» Grains: including oats, pasta, rice, rye, maize, millet
» Grain products: including biscuits, bread, cakes, crackers, pastry
» Honey
» Maple syrup
» Starchy vegetables: including potatoes, yams, and sweetcorn
» Sugar and sweets

GROUP 3: Non-starchy vegetables and fats

» Butter, cream
» Herbs, spices, seasonings
» Olive and other oils
» Salads
» Seeds

GROUP 4: Fruit

» All varieties

FOOD COMBINING CHART

YES	NO
» Groups 1 and 3	» Groups 1 and 2
» Groups 2 and 3	» Groups 1 and 4
» Group 4 alone	» Groups 2 and 4
	» Groups 3 and 4

Tips on food combining

» Always eat fruit by itself, 30 minutes before other food
groups and, ideally, first thing in the morning on an
empty stomach.
» Leave two hours after a carbohydrate meal before eating
a dense protein meal.
» Leave three hours after a protein meal before eating
carbohydrates.
» Beans and pulses have a mixture of starch and protein,
predominantly starch. You can combine most pulses and
beans with grains as well as salads and vegetables.

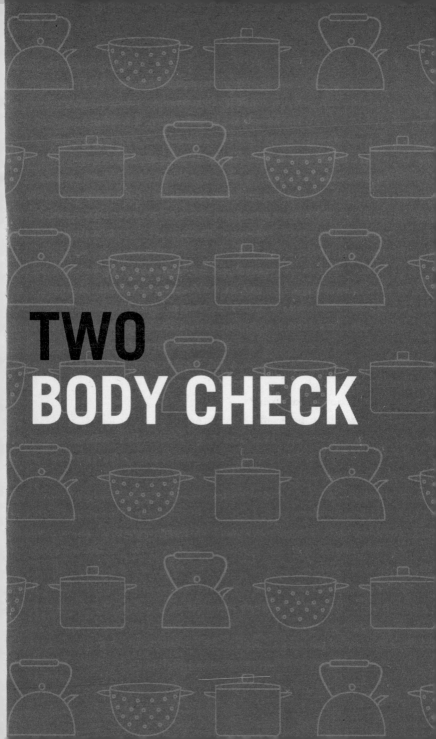

TWO
BODY CHECK

All the recipes in this book are simply very good for you. However, it's also great to have a sense of just how healthy, or perhaps I should say unhealthy, you are. In the original book *You Are What You Eat* I included a big chapter on getting to know your body. Here I've included a quick questionnaire that will give you a good idea of how you're doing on the McKeith scale of healthy living. Some of my questions are quite specific to help you with your body check; perhaps you're mega stressed, or you need to detox. If that's the case I'll point you in the direction of some great recipes which are perfect for you. As always, I advise that if you are considering a radical change of diet, you should consult your GP first – especially if you are pregnant, elderly or under 16.

GETTING TO GRIPS WITH YOU: DR GILLIAN DIET CHECK

All of my clients are required to keep a record of everything that they eat and drink for a week. I recommend that you do the same. You may surprise yourself and learn a lot about your habits. You just might see that you are not eating as well as you had convinced yourself or that you may be eating the same things every day. Alternatively you may find out that things are actually looking good. Either way, you will be more aware of you and what you put into your body.

ANSWER THE FOLLOWING QUESTIONS WITH A YES OR NO:

01 Do you drink a minimum of 2 litres of still (mineral or filtered) water a day?

02 Do you eat fresh fruit and vegetables every day?

03 Do you eat essential fats in the form of fish, avocados, nuts, seeds or cold-pressed oils on a regular basis every week?

04 Do you avoid foods containing preservatives, additives, sugar and salt?

05 Do you cook from scratch rather than using tins and packets?

06 Do you eat a range of whole grains such as millet, oats, brown rice, rye, quinoa and barley, rather than white, refined grains?

07 Do you eat a non-sugary breakfast every day?

08 Do you eat pulses, such as chickpeas, beans and lentils at least 3 times a week or more?

09 Do you choose organically grown foods where possible?

10 Do you avoid fizzy drinks, regular tea, coffee and alcohol?

11 Do you eat a healthy lunch each day?

12 Do you eat a healthy dinner before 7:30pm each day?

ADD UP YOUR YES ANSWERS. THIS IS YOUR SCORE.

» **10 or more**
YOU ARE LIKE A DR GILLIAN GROUPIE!
You are definitely in my 'good books'. I am proud of you so well done! It looks like you are really making an effort. You and your body will benefit now and in the future so please keep it up. You're going to get a real buzz from my Veggie Vitality Juice (p.68) and I hope you discover lots of new recipes in this book which you might not have tried before. The key for you is to keep your healthy food choices as varied as possible for ultimate nutrition.

» **Between 6 and 9**
COULD TRY HARDER
When it comes to your body and good health, you know that I believe half-measures to be unacceptable, and you should feel this too. The bottom line is that you probably don't feel 100 per cent, so either do it right or not at all. Get on track now. You'll be happier, with a much healthier

body and a far sexier one too. You'll thank me for it. I'm
sure you're no stranger to lettuce but perhaps you need
some more exciting ideas – check out Crunchy Walnut
Coleslaw (p.117), Tabbouleh (p.120) or even my Seaweed
Salad (p.129). And if you need a bit of convincing that
beans are far from boring, try the Aduki Bean Stew (p.157)
with Onion Gravy (p.221). Top it with my healthy Millet
Mash (p.158).

Go for it.

» Less than 6
ON A SLIPPERY SLOPE
I doubt you are even close to experiencing optimum health
and vitality. I urge you to start out with the smoothies
and take each day at a time. You will love my Mango Mania
(p.75). Once you have tried that, you will be hooked. Also
try the Quick Bites (pp.180–193), which don't take much
time at all. Just think how different things could be if you
allowed yourself to be McKeith'd. Read the Food Philosophy
chapter, specifically the section Embrace Change (p.16).
As a special treat to get started, get a friend or a loved one
to make one of my recipes for you. I have found that for
people who are finding the transition from an unhealthy
to healthy diet difficult my Chicken Burgers (p.139) with
Raw Salsa (p.204) and a crunchy green salad of mange
tout, fennel, celery, carrot and beetroot are perfect.
Shepherdess Pie (p.143) is our family favourite. Some
very easy changes will make a huge difference. So take
that important first step.

IMMUNE SYSTEM CHECK

The foods you eat are like a tonic to the immune system.
Certain foods can suppress immune function while the
right foods may actually boost immune activity. For example,
sprouted broccoli seeds have been shown to be one of the most
powerful immune-boosting foods that we know of. Conversely,
people who eat high quantities of foods with refined sugars
often suffer from allergies, food intolerances, chemical
sensitivities, hay fever, colds, flu, headaches, and other
disorders, all of which are related to immune dysfunction.
In our modern world, immune degradation is becoming
a prevalent issue among the mass population at large.

ANSWER YES OR NO:

01 Do you have bad breath?

02 Do you suffer from congestion or a runny nose?

03 Does your tongue have a thick, white or yellow coating
or teeth marks round the side?

04 Do you have dark circles under your eyes?

05 Do you have white spots on your nails?

06 Do you have pain or sensitivity under the right rib area?

07 Do you have thrush or yeast problems?

08 Are you tired all the time?

09 Do you catch colds or flus frequently?

10 Do you suffer from hayfever, allergies or food sensitivities?

ADD UP YOUR YES ANSWERS TO FIND OUT YOUR SCORE.
» Between 7 and 10
IMMUNE BASKETCASE
You urgently need to comply with everything that
I tell you. Do not miss my Carrot and Almond Soup (p.96),
which is a really easy place to start. Carrots are high in
the antioxidant Beta Carotene and Vitamins A and D. Eat
sprouted seeds (p.42) and get into fruit because of the high
vitamin content. Pineapple is a great source of vitamin C,
for example. Grilled Banana With Citrus Spice (p.214) is
a delicious fruit treat and for breakfast, road test my fruit
salads (p.86). If you feel the onset of a cold or the flu, try
using cinnamon in your juices and smoothies (pp.65–81),
or in herbal teas (pp.51–54). Cinnamon has a historical
use of providing relief when faced with these symptoms,
especially when mixed in a tea with some fresh ginger.

» Between 4 and 6
MESS WAITING TO HAPPEN
Act before it's too late. Whenever you feel under par, make
a Sprout Surprise Juice (p.69). You will love my immune
boosting Baked Salmon with Spinach and Leeks (p.147).
There's lots of fresh ginger in this dish, which is beneficial
for the immune system, and spinach, which is a good source
of another immune booster, Co Q 10. This recipe also has
lots of onions – it's important to eat lots of onions (and
garlic). I once had a friend who worked in an onion and
garlic factory. He said that in the entire time he worked

in the onion job, he never once had a cold! Several anti-inflammatory agents in onions render them helpful with the respiratory congestion associated with the common cold. Both onions and garlic also contain compounds that may help reduce inflammation. In addition, the quercitin and other flavonoids found in onions work with vitamin C to help kill harmful bacteria, making onions an especially good addition to soups and stews during cold and flu season.

» Between 1 and 3

HOPEFUL

There's still a little work to be done, but you could lift yourself up fairly quickly. You should eat lots of powerful sprouted broccoli seeds whenever you get the chance. And start growing your own sprouted seeds too. Commit to making 2–3 vegetable juices (pp.67–71) every week, thus delivering lots of nutrients to your immune system. I have a client who used to live on crisps and burgers and now her favourite recipe is the Fennel Fun juice (p.71). Also, try my Sea Vegetable and Sprouts Salad (p.121) and don't miss out on the immune boosting Raw Avocado and Cucumber Soup (p.106).

TOXIN CHECK

Some people load themselves with unhealthy food choices that are difficult to digest. This creates toxins. Such toxins may strip the body of much needed nutrients.

ARE YOU A TOXIC LOADER?

01 Do you add table salt to your cooking and/or to food before you have even tasted it?

02 Do you add sugar to your tea or coffee?

03 Do you drink caffeinated tea, coffee, tap water, diet drinks or fizzy drinks regularly?

04 Do you eat packaged foods laden with preservatives or chemicals that you cannot pronounce?

05 Do you eat such processed, packaged or microwaveable meals more than 3 times weekly?

06 Do you drink more than the recommended units of alcohol (14 for women and 21 for men) every week or binge drink on weekends?

07 Are you a takeaway junkie?

08 Do you suffer from continual headaches?

09 Do you have spots or acne anywhere on your skin or do you suffer from hives or have hemorrhoids?

10 Do you smoke cigarettes or use recreational drugs?

ADD UP YOUR YES ANSWERS TO FIND OUT YOUR SCORE.

» **Between 8 and 10**

TOXIC WASTE DUMP

If you continue down this route, you might as well take the exit right now because I can't help you. You had better either do it my way or it's the highway for you. The first thing you must do is make my simple and detoxifying Veggie Virgin juice (p.67). It tastes delicious, absolutely scrumptious. But to truly get on the detox drive, you cannot miss the Mung Bean Casserole (p.177) with Gourmet Brown Rice (p.185) and a crunchy salad. It's the best dish ever for ridding the body of nasty toxins and bacteria. So many of the TV participants have told me how this recipe has put them on the road to healthy eating. If they can do it, you can too.

» **Between 5 and 7**

PRETTY PUTRID

Start juicing my vegetable concoctions right away, especially Fennel Fun (p.71) and Total Cleanser (p.66) to give you a clean out. This is the most incredible detoxification tonic.

» **Between 2 and 4**

TOXIC TEASER

You are teetering in either direction. Instead of going downhill, keep going in my direction. Turn on to crunchy salads (pp.116–132) as you need lots of food enzymes. Toxic types are often deficient in good, healthy essential fats and minerals. Redress the balance with a big Green Salad (p.128) and also try the Spring Salad with hemp seeds (p.119), a fantastic source of essential fats.

THE TONGUE CHECK

Your tongue is a very telling indicator of how healthy
your diet is.

01 Does your tongue have a line down the middle?

02 Does your tongue have teeth marks round the side?

03 Does your tongue have a bright red tip?

04 Is your tongue sore?

05 Does your tongue appear dotted all over?

**IF YOU ANSWER YES TO A PARTICULAR QUESTION,
IT COULD MEAN:**

01 Weak digestion. You may feel bloated and suffer from
gas or indigestion. A strong digestive system is important
for nutrient absorption. I would suggest food combining for
a period of eight weeks (see pp.18–19). Keep meals simple,
and ingredients that are particularly good for you include
brown rice, avocado and tofu. Try the Avocado and Barley
Salad (p.116), Smoked Tofu and Bean Burgers (p.155),
Tofu with Steamed Vegetables (p.169) and Gourmet
Brown Rice (p.185).

02 Spleen weakness and nutrient deficiencies. Your
spleen is your energy battery and may not be taking up
nutrients as effectively as it should. Symptoms can include
feeling tired all the time, gassy and bloated. Aduki Bean

Stew (p.157) is a good digestion strengthener, so don't miss out on this. And look for recipes that contain beetroot (p.99), celery, fennel (p.71), dill (p.163), chicken (p.141), garlic, kidney beans (p.175), parsley (p.120), pumpkins (p.100) and turnips (p.98).

03 A red tip may indicate either emotional upset or that your body is stressed. Either way, you will need B vitamins to calm it all down. Foods rich in B vitamins include brown rice and other wholesome grains, root vegetables and beans. Go for my Haricot Bean Loaf (p.145), Mediterranean Black-Eye Pea Casserole (p.146), Chickpea Burgers (p.138) and Gourmet Brown Rice (p.185).

04 A sore tongue may indicate a vitamin B6 deficiency, and could also indicate that niacin and/or iron levels are low. Drink nettle or dandelion teas (pp.51–52) and eat foods rich in vitamin B6, including sunflower seeds, brown rice, buckwheat and avocados. Try my Juicy Smoothie (p.81), Tabbouleh (p.120) and Breakfast Soup Blitz (p.88). Best Ever Beetroot Soup (p.99) should regularly be on the menu in your house too.

05 This can be a sign of what I call liver stagnation. In western holistic medicine, we think of the liver as the organ of detoxification. The liver tries to keep toxins out of your blood stream, particularly those that come into your body via your diet. When your liver is overworked, it may perform sluggishly. In the West this is often called a congested liver. Foods that support the liver are good for everyone, and include cruciferous veggies such as kohlrabi (p.117), broccoli (p.131), cauliflower (p.112); flax seeds (p.89), hemp seeds (p.100) and sunflower seeds. Nettle and dandelion teas help too (pp.51–52). White Bean and Cabbage Soup is a must (p.101).

THREE
GETTING
ORGANIZED

When you're struggling to cope with a hectic job, a home and a family, organization is the key. I once learned a hard lesson about being organized.

Years ago, when I was a student, my friend and I left the house one afternoon, and returned to find the front door ajar. Afraid we'd been burgled we called the police, who came to our rescue. One of the constables ran into the house and came out moments later with the words, 'The house has been ransacked. He said the kitchen had been the worst hit, but when I walked into the room with him, it was so embarrassing. Nothing had been stolen. The mess that surrounded me was nothing to do with burglars; this was just the way I kept my kitchen back then. From that moment on, I vowed to get my life in order. The following pages contain my 10 steps to get it together.

10 STEPS TO GET IT TOGETHER

1. KEEP A TIDY KITCHEN

The kitchen represents the focal point of the home and the centre of our lives – after all, it's here that we feed our bodies with fuel to thrive. And since food is a major component of life, the kitchen is a critical space in the house, or at least it should be. A tidy kitchen means a tidy mind, a tidy body and a tidy you. Get your kitchen in order and you will soon find your whole life follows suit. OK, so maybe you think I am overstating this. But I want you to go and get your kitchen in order. Today! Get rid of all that rubbish, including those useless papers, tape dispensers, paper clips, old birthday cards and more that you've been hoarding in that drawer. Just do it, and see the difference in your home, your mind and your life. It's a great start to everything we need to do together here.

2. GET RID OF JUNK FOODS

The first step towards healthy eating is choosing healthy ingredients. Start by throwing out salty convenience foods, fatty foods, sugary drinks, chemical snacks, foods with unpronounceable ingredients you can't decipher, hydrogenated oils and processed junk food from your fridge and cupboards.

3. SHOP IN THE RIGHT FRAME OF MIND

Never shop when you're hungry – you'll end up loading your trolley with sugar-rich but nutrient-poor convenience foods such as pies, crisps, sweets, cakes, biscuits and desserts, all of which should be limited on a healthy eating plan. Have a clear idea of what you are going to eat and the ingredients you need – you'll be less likely to make unhealthy choices. Take this book with you if it helps – that way you'll have quick and easy access to my recipes and their ingredients. It'll be as if I'm with you, helping you out!

4. CHANGE YOUR SNACK MINDSET

Stop thinking of quick snacks as sugary flapjacks, biscuits, chocolates, crisps and other nasties. Start associating fast, on-the-run snacks with easy, healthy alternatives. In the morning, for example, grab a couple of whole peppers, a whole cucumber and a celery stick. Wash them, throw it in a bag and voilà, you have your morning and afternoon snacks for the day. Eat the pepper whole, in the same way as you would an apple. Just hold it in your hand and bite into it. This is the new way of snacking with whole vegetables – you don't have to spend all that time and energy slicing them. It's faster, easier and healthier. See chapter 10 for lots of easy snack recipes and ideas (pp.194–209).

5. MAKE GOOD USE OF YOUR FRIDGE/FREEZER

Make sure you know how to make the most of your freezer. Did you, for example, know that you can freeze fresh herbs? Or that freezing grains will prevent moulds and beasties from taking over them? Think of your freezer as a form of natural preservative. Keep your perishables in there and bring them out to the larder or fridge on the week you want to use them.

Most fridge-freezers are the size of postage stamps and are usually at feet level. Half the time you can't get down there to see what's in them unless you have a good back, strong knees and exceptional eyesight. So, if you ever have any spare cash, go out and buy the biggest fridge-freezer you can find.

6. STOCK UP ON KITCHEN EQUIPMENT

While travelling the country with the TV series *You Are What You Eat*, I've noticed that most people don't have enough basic items of kitchen equipment, such as sharp knives, or a good range of pots, plates and mixing bowls.

Here's my list of kitchen equipment essentials:

- baking trays
- large casserole dish
- measuring jug
- metal grater
- peeler
- plastic chopping board for fish
- scales
- set of saucepans
- set of sharp knives
- thick wooden chopping board
- wok
- wooden spoons

Some extra must-haves

When you have these items, the sky's the limit with how creative you can be:

- food processor (apart from everything else, it will blend, whisk and turn nuts into a fluffy whipped cream)
- blender (for your morning fruit smoothies and blended smooth soups)
- juicer (for your fruit or vegetable juices)
- And if you really want to treat yourself, buy a spiralizer. This is my most recent kitchen discovery and I love it. It's an amazing gadget that can make delicious raw spaghetti from any root vegetable. Sounds crazy, but when you apply it to butternut squash, beetroots or sweet potato, you end up with a food that tastes like spaghetti, looks like spaghetti and has a similar consistency and texture to spaghetti. It's almost hard to believe that you are not eating pasta but in fact raw root vegetables full of food enzymes. Your kids will just gobble up this new form of uncooked pasta without the refined flour of regular white pasta.

Getting organized

7. DON'T BE AFRAID OF HEALTH FOOD SHOPS

Years ago, when I was a student at Edinburgh University, I had a boyfriend who was a health food junkie. I thought he was a bit strange in those days eating tofu (instead of meat), bean chips (instead of crisps) and blackstrap molasses (instead of sugar). But it must have been working in his favour: his body was in impeccable condition. He's the one who first introduced me to the world of health food shops and got me hooked.

Health food shops generally tend to be the pioneers for many products that eventually make their way on to supermarket shelves. This was exactly what happened with yogurt, for example. When it first came on to the market years ago, it was only available in health food shops, but, over time it proved to be a big seller, and began to be stocked by supermarkets. It was exactly the same with brown rice, tofu, rice milk, and even soy sauce.

My point here is that you need not fear health food shops. It's true, when you first go into one many of the foods may seem strange and unusual. But, remember, many of those weird-sounding foods could soon become the regular foods that we all buy from the supermarket.

Health food shops often stock healthy alternatives to conventional products, for example, biscuits with no added sugar, or healthy alternatives to meat and animal proteins, such as tofu and tempeh. I've even found alternative juice drinks sweetened with apple juice instead of sugar; sugar-free corn flakes; salt-free vegetable bouillon powders for making soups; bouquets of dried powdered herbal seasonings as salt alternatives, and so on.

Health food shops pride themselves on carrying products that are healthy, organic, and contain no chemicals, no preservatives and no artificial ingredients. They carry many products with particular health benefits such as sea vegetables or seaweeds, beans, grains, pulses, seeds and nuts, vitamin, mineral and superfood supplements and herbal teas. So have no fear, health foods are here!

8. FOLLOW THESE HEALTHY SHOPPING GUIDELINES

The major supermarkets should have at least 90 per cent or more of the foods mentioned here. You can also fill in at farmers' markets and health food shops or websites (www.drgillianmckeith.com).

» Load up on fresh fruits, vegetables and sprouted seeds.

» Buy fresh fish – preferably white or oily. If you must eat red meat, buy fresh, organic lean meat, which is much more nutritious than sausages, pies and processed meats.

» Avoid fruit juices made with sugar and preservatives and go for fresh, unsweetened juices instead.

» When buying dairy produce avoid full-fat milk and yogurt and go for low-fat dairy products, or skimmed or grain milks such as spelt milk, almond milk, amaranth milk, oat milk or rice milk.

» Choose softer cheeses such as goat, cottage cheese and ricotta instead of hard cheese.

» Avoid ready-made meals, convenience foods, and canned foods containing salt, sugar and preservatives. They are likely to be low in nutrients and high in calories, additives and chemicals.

9. STOCK UP ON STAPLES

The following items are store cupboard essentials and
staples for your kitchen. Most of them are available
in supermarkets or health food shops.

» **Dried Herbs**

I love fresh herbs most of all and use them liberally
in my cooking and salads (see p. 48). But dried herbs
can come in handy for seasoning too. Buy the following
organic dried herbs:

» Basil	» Mint
» Bay leaves	» Oregano
» Dill	» Rosemary
» Fennel	» Tarragon
» Fenugreek	» Thyme
» Garlic	

» **Spices**

» Cinnamon (ground)	» Mustard seeds
» Cloves	» Nutmeg
» Coriander seeds	» Saffron
» Cumin (ground)	» Turmeric
» Ginger	

» **Flavourings (savoury)**

» Agar-agar flakes (neutral-tasting seaweed
which provides jelly like consistency perfect
for healthy desserts)
» Almond powder
» Bouillon powder or vegetable stock cubes
» Brown rice vinegar
» Capers
» Cider vinegar
» Mirin

- >> Miso paste (a fantastic way to flavour foods – try all the different types, from the meaty hatcho miso to the lighter white misos)
- >> Nori flakes
- >> Seaweed flake seasonings
- >> Seaweeds
- >> Sesame sauce
- >> Shoyu soy sauce
- >> Tahini
- >> Tamari (wheat-free soya) sauce
- >> Umeboshi paste
- >> Umeboshi plum seasoning

- >> **Flavourings (sweet)**
- >> Apple juice
- >> Barley malt syrup
- >> Brown rice syrup
- >> Carob powder
- >> Date syrup or date paste (you can make your own date paste by blending fresh dates and water together in the blender)
- >> Grain milks (rice, soya, oat, spelt, amaranth, millet and almond)
- >> Maple syrup
- >> Vanilla bean pod
- >> Vanilla extract

» Nuts and seeds

Nuts and seeds are power-packed with nutrients and
healthy, good fat. They are best eaten in moderation,
but I thoroughly recommend a small handful as a snack.
Alternatively, sprinkle them whole on cereals or chopped
on salads and soups. Because of their high fat content,
nuts and seeds only keep at room temperature for
about a month (in an airtight container in dark, cool
cupboard), but will keep for four months in the fridge
and eight months in the freezer. If you find nuts hard
to digest, try soaking them in water overnight.

- » Almond
- » Cashew
- » Flax seeds
- » Hemp seeds
- » Pine nut
- » Pumpkin seeds
- » Sunflower seeds
- » Brazil nut
- » Chestnut
- » Hazelnut
- » Pecan
- » Pistachio
- » Sesame seeds
- » Walnut

» Sprouted seeds

Sprouts are nutritional stars. They are fantastic immunity-
boosters, being high in antioxidants, vitamins, minerals,
protein, enzymes and fibre. You can buy them in health
food shops or even try sprouting your own (see my previous
book *You Are What You Eat*). Always eat these sprouts
raw, whether in salads or added to hot savoury dishes
just before serving.

- » Alfalfa
- » Clover
- » Mung beans
- » Broccoli seeds
- » Lentils

» Oils

Always get cold-pressed nut and seed oils.

» Avocado	» Hemp
» Olive	» Pumpkin
» Sesame	» Sunflower
» Walnut	

» Beans and pulses

Beans are rich in essential nutrients, high in fibre and are a source of good, healthy fat. Research has shown that a regular intake of beans can help lower cholesterol levels and the risks of heart attack, and may help inhibit the growth of cancer cells. Beans are a very good source of protein, but with the exception of soy beans (which are a complete protein) they need to be eaten with grains to form a complete protein that the body can readily absorb. Beans are incredibly versatile when it comes to creating recipes and I am a huge fan. Store dried beans in an airtight container at room temperature and they will keep almost indefinitely. Keep fresh beans in perforated plastic bags in the fridge crisper section; edible pod beans will keep for three to five days, shell beans for two to three days.

» Aduki	» Black bean
» Black-eye pea	» Broad bean
» Butter bean	» Cannellini
» Chickpea	» Flageolet
» Haricot	» Kidney bean
» Lentil	» Mung beans
» Soybean	» Split pea

» Tempeh

You'll find tempeh in health food shops in the fridge section. Made from soybeans, tempeh provides a good supply of B vitamins. It's a very nutritious substitute for meat.

» Tofu

Try the different types. The silky soft one is great for sauces; the firmer ones are best for snacks or stews.

» Miso

Miso is a fermented soybean paste and is packed with immune-supporting minerals and energy boosting B vitamins. You can find it in paste or powder form in health food shops and it's a valuable addition to your kitchen cupboard. There are many varieties, ranging from light to dark, a taste for every palate. Try my Ten-Minute Miso Fish Soup (p.103) for an instant pick-me-up.

» Flours

You won't need all these flours but it's good to know what's out there. Just pick one or two.

» Hemp	» Millet
» Oat	» Potato
» Quinoa	» Rice
» Soy	» Sunflower seed
» Wholewheat	

» Grains

Grains are your basic energy food. I always recommend unrefined grains, which are not only a good source of complex carbohydrate, but also fibre, B vitamins, vitamin E, calcium, magnesium, potassium, iron, zinc, copper and selenium. Research shows that a diet rich in unrefined grains can help lower cholesterol and regulate blood sugar levels. Grains provide the perfect accompaniment to all my bean dishes, and they make delicious and fulfilling meals out of salads. Store whole grains in airtight containers away from heat, light and moisture. Different grains have different storage times, so be sure to check. You can store grains for longer in the fridge or freezer.

» Amaranth
» Basmati rice
» Buckwheat
» Cous-cous
» Oats
» Spelt
» Barley
» Brown rice
» Bulgar
» Millet
» Quinoa

» Fruit

Fruits are packed with nutrients. Eat a wide variety of fruits to ensure a variety of goodness, from the B vitamins, folate and potassium in bananas (a nutritious energy boost alternative to sweets) to the high levels of vitamin C in citrus fruits such as lemons and limes. Dried fruits like dates and figs are a good source of fibre (and a yummy snack), while dark orange fruits (apricots, peaches and mangoes) are rich in antioxidants. Far and away the nutrient winners are the berry fruits, including strawberries, raspberries, blackberries, blueberries, cherries and cranberries. Berries are rich in bioflavonoids, which have powerful antioxidant, anti-infective and anti-inflammatory properties. They literally help the body to resist illness. Remember that it's not a good idea to combine fruit with other food groups (see p.19). It's an excellent idea to eat just one type of fruit, for example a punnet of blueberries or raspberries. But also try out my fab fruit salads (p.86).

›› **Vegetables**

Eat lots of dark green leafy vegetables, such as kale, cabbage or broccoli, and alliums, such as garlic, onions or leeks, at least once a day. Fresh, raw vegetables are rich in phytochemicals, which can be beneficial to your heart, skin, hair, mental, reproductive and overall health. Eat lots of the following vegetables too.

- ›› Asparagus
- ›› Cabbage
- ›› Cauliflower
- ›› Garlic
- ›› Leeks
- ›› Onions
- ›› Peas (green)
- ›› Rocket
- ›› Spinach
- ›› Tomatoes
- ›› Turnips
- ›› Yams
- ›› Broccoli
- ›› Carrots
- ›› Celery
- ›› Kale
- ›› Mustard greens
- ›› Parsley
- ›› Peppers
- ›› Romaine lettuce
- ›› Sweet potatoes
- ›› Turnip greens
- ›› Watercress

» Superfood supplements

It might be a good idea to add a multi-vitamin and mineral supplement to your shopping basket to help correct nutritional deficiencies and protect against the nutrient-depleting effects of stress, poor diet and environmental toxins. Following are the key supplements I would recommend that you take every day for constitutional support.

» Supplement basket

My supplement basket often consists of green superfoods as follows:

» Liquid algae (which I squirt into my mouth because it's like a nutrient shot of minerals)

» Spirulina tablets or powder for my smoothies

» Dr Gillian McKeith's Living Food Energy Powder formulation for a complete nutritional foundation (use in smoothies too)

» Aloe vera juice for healthy bowels and digestive tract (preferably non-bitter)

10. COOK IN THE RAW

I always advise my clients to include raw foods in the same meal when they prepare cooked foods. This is because raw foods contain food enzymes that are essential for optimum digestion and general wellbeing. Adding raw vegetables, raw seeds or raw nuts is a great way of taking in food enzymes. Just think of them as 'Digestive Dynamos'.

HERBS

Herbs make truly fantastic natural flavourings – you won't miss salt if you use them! Be passionate. Feel free to use generous proportions when using them in cooking. Experiment to your heart's content and discover your true favourites. Most herbs have healing properties, and these green plants also contain an abundance of minerals, so you'll see lots used in my recipes. Here are some of my favourite herbs:

Basil

Basil has a cooling quality, which means it can help to neutralize harmful acids in the gut. This sweet-tasting herb has been used for years as a calming aid for indigestion. It tastes great in salads. My favourite!

Bay

Bay leaves add great flavour to soups, stews, sauces and stock (but remember not to actually eat them). They are also thought to help with gas, headaches and indigestion.

Chervil

Chervil has a unique flavour that's a little like parsley with a hint of aniseed. It is thought to help stimulate and ease digestion. It has such a wonderful flavour that it can take a simple dish and turn it into a gourmet delicacy.

Chives

Numerous studies have linked plants like chives to helping lower and prevent hypertension. Chives are also rich in vitamin C and iron. Chives are the perfect companion to cucumber (see p.106 for my Raw Avocado and Cucumber Soup).

Coriander

In herbalism, coriander is known as an 'alterative', which simply means it can help purify the blood. Coriander also helps the body absorb nutrients and remove waste matter. I often add coriander to recipes that include beans because of its ability to assist digestion.

Dill

Dill is a warming herb and a good source of fibre, iron, magnesium and calcium. Another top choice for me. It can be strengthening to the spleen, liver and stomach organs. I use dill in salads, soups, casseroles and even in my Hearty Lentil Stew (see p.163). It works like a charm.

Lovage

I love this herb. Its aromatic elements are similar to those in celery and it will add real zip to your dishes. It's also a diuretic and thus a good addition to any weight loss programme. Lovage is great simply thrown into any soup just before serving.

Oregano

Oregano has an antioxidant punch (remember, antioxidants are powerful allies in helping to prevent cancer, heart disease and stroke). Its antioxidant properties are partly due to the presence of rosmarinic acid, an antibacterial, antiviral and antioxidant compound. Oregano goes wonderfully well with tomatoes so it's perfect for marinades, stews and tomato sauces.

Parsley

Parsley is the culinary multivitamin, a nutrient powerhouse. It is a good source of beta carotene, calcium and more vitamin C than citrus fruits. This is one of the most important plants for providing vitamins to the body. It helps the body's defensive mechanisms and this may help keep negative bacteria at bay. If you warm parsley slightly, its flavour will soften and adapt nicely to whatever food you are preparing, so you can use this herb in just about any savoury dish. It's very nourishing and restoring, and can help neutralize the intense flavour of garlic on the breath.

Rosemary

Rosemary contains properties that can help support the immune system. It's also thought to increase blood flow to the head and brain, increasing concentration and improving memory. I love to add a few sprigs while roasting vegetables, but remember not to eat the twigs.

Tarragon

This strong aniseed-perfumed herb contains compounds that are believed to help lower blood pressure. When added to a dish it's best used in moderation because of the intense flavour, but it's delicious with chicken or fish, and in stews.

Thyme

Thyme is considered a healing herb and is particularly good for chest and respiratory problems. It has antiseptic properties too. So adding fresh thyme to your salad dressing not only enhances flavour but also adds nutrients.

HERBAL TEAS

I'm a big fan of herbal teas, which I love for their soothing, healing and revitalizing properties. There are three ways you can enjoy these fabulous natural concoctions. Of course you could grow your own. I'm lucky to have a back garden, where I grow some herbs myself – I use the leaves, flowers, roots, or even the whole plant, depending on how I feel – but a window box will do! If you can't be bothered with the business of growing, you can buy the dried leaves from a specialist herbal shop – or, for a really easy life, just buy herbal teabags from a health food shop or supermarket.

Try my list of favourite teas below, and as you get to know the different varieties and their health benefits, learn to listen to what your body is telling you. You'll soon sense which tea you need on any one particular day – the cleansing powers of dandelion, say, or the stress-busting qualities of linden flowers. You'll be amazed at the results!

Nettle: my number one favourite

If there's one herbal tea you should reach for, this is it. All my clients know it's my staple favourite. It's loaded with minerals and iron, which makes it an excellent blood-builder – in fact, it's a tonic for the whole body. Personally, I always feel energized after drinking nettle tea, so I make sure I sit down to a cuppa a few times a week. Although nettle is not a laxative, it's such a great system-cleanser that two to three cups a day can get your bowels going nicely.

Note to men: Nettle isn't just a woman's herb. Studies have shown that this plant may also help to prevent prostate problems.

Dandelion: the liver-cleanser

This herb is readily available. I've often gone out with my daughters and collected lovely yellow-flowered dandelions, which we then soak in warm water to make a delicious tea. That's how easy it can be. Dandelion is a fantastic liver-cleanser, and can help to clear toxins from the body. It's also a diuretic, which means it can assist with fluid retention and weight loss. To make your own dandelion tea from fresh leaves simply pour just boiled water over a small bunch of leaves, steep for 10 minutes and then strain before drinking.

Linden flower: the stress-buster

Linden flower tea can be effective in calming the nervous system and helping to induce sleep. If you suffer from that on-edge feeling, this is a good gentle tea for you.

Mullein: the mucus-mover

If you have mucus or bronchial congestion, hayfever, earaches caused by excessive mucus, a hacking cough or sinusitis, then start drinking this tea – fast!

Pau d'arco: the yeast-fighter

Pau d'arco is antibacterial, antiviral and antifungal. So, if you suffer from thrush, digestive problems or general poor immunity, including frequent colds or flu, drink this tea. As soon as autumn ends, I load up on stocks of it for the winter!

Fresh mint: a digestive dynamo

Peppermint tea is refreshing, energizing and soothing to the tummy. If you have a line down the middle of your tongue, which may suggest stomach weakness, then this should become your top tea.

If you want the real thing, then buy a small mint plant from a supermarket or local garden centre. Just clip off some fresh leaves, put them into a cup or pot of water, let it sit for a few minutes, and then drink. Bliss!

The great thing about mint tea is that you can get it in restaurants, too – whether teabags or fresh leaves.

Slippery elm: nature's anti-inflammatory

This tea can soothe inflamed mucous membranes in the stomach, bowels and urinary tract. Use it for diarrhoea and ulcers, and for the treatment of colds, flu and sore throats.

Red clover: the blood-purifier

Think of this tea as the antioxidant powerhouse. I sometimes use it for my clients on their detox days.

Lemon balm: the mood-lifter

Lemon balm has long been used as a mood-lifter and nerve-soother. It may also relieve tummy upsets and gas.

Hawthorn: the heart-helper

A must-have for anyone who has a history of or family predisposition to heart ailments such as high blood pressure, hardening of the arteries, angina, high cholesterol and varicose veins. Hawthorn has also been shown to improve circulation to the extremities.

Other great herbal teas include:

- Bilberry
- Camomile
- Elderflower
- Fennel
- Ginger
- Green
- Jasmine
- Juniper berry
- Lemongrass
- Licorice
- Passionflower
- Raspberry leaf
- Red clover
- Sage
- Spearmint

Ask Yourself: What do I feel like eating today? Which bean, which herb, which veggies, which seasonings?

SPICES AND NATURAL FLAVOURINGS

Spices and other natural foods have been used for centuries for their medicinal as well as their culinary qualities. Researchers are continuing to study the healing properties that can be offered by these natural remedies even today. They taste great, but don't go overboard with them – over-spicy food can irritate the lining of the stomach, so cut down on extra-hot curries and chillies and go for the gentler spices instead:

Cardamom (medium)

Cardamom contains essential oil properties and its main use is as a spice in coffees, curries and other Asian and Middle Eastern foods. Available as pods and seeds, it has a pungent eucalyptus-like taste. Medicinally it is used as an aid to digestion. It is also thought to help colds, bronchitis, fevers, inflammatory conditions and liver complaints.

Cinnamon (mild)

Available in stick and powder form, cinnamon makes a great addition to desserts and Middle Eastern savoury dishes. It is often used as an antidote to diarrhoea and stomach upsets.

Cumin (mild)

Research has shown that cumin may stimulate the secretion of pancreatic enzymes, compounds necessary for proper digestion and nutrient assimilation. The seeds may also have anti-carcinogenic properties. I use cumin, along with turmeric, in my Mung Bean Casserole (see p.177) – it gives real character to the dish. A great spice for detoxing.

Fennel bulb (mild)

The aniseed-y aroma of this bulb is one of my favourites. Delicious raw or cooked, it is an excellent source of fibre. It is also believed to be helpful in lowering elevated cholesterol levels as well as the diarrhoea and constipation that are symptomatic of irritable bowel syndrome.

Fenugreek (strong)

Fenugreek is one of the oldest known medicinal plants. Its dietary and medicinal uses date back to the ancient Egyptians, and today it is often used in Asian dishes. Fenugreek has always been valued for its health benefits – most commonly used to help manage diabetes and obesity.

Garlic (strong)

Regular consumption of garlic can help lower high blood pressure and cholesterol levels. Its pungent flavour makes a delicious addition to virtually any savoury dish, particularly pasta and stews.

Ginger (strong)

Ginger speeds metabolic rate. It's also a warming food that's perfect for veggie juices in the winter, good for colds and nausea, and is even said to help with mild depression. It happens to taste fantastic too.

Horseradish (strong)

Horseradish is a relative of the mustard family that acts as a digestive stimulant. Some people tell me it's great for clearing a blocked nose too!

Nutmeg (mild)

Like other spices, nutmeg has aromatic, stimulant, and carminative properties. It has been used with advantage in mild cases of diarrhoea, flatulent colic, and certain forms of dyspepsia. Good in sweet and savoury dishes.

Saffron (mild)
The dried stamens of a crocus flower, and said to be the most expensive spice in the world, saffron is used in many European and Asian dishes. It is believed to aid digestion, and relieves stomach upsets and tension.

Turmeric (mild)
Turmeric is an antioxidant that neutralizes free radicals and therefore may help to protect against cancer. It is also an anti-inflammatory and may help to protect the liver from a variety of toxins. Indian doctors have used turmeric to treat many ailments, from sprains to jaundice. I use it in my Mung Bean Casserole (see p.177)

Vanilla (mild)
Vanilla is an aromatic stimulant that is thought to have aphrodisiac qualities. It's a wonderful spice for sweetening without sugar. Use the pod or essence.

If you can't take the heat
If hot spices don't agree with you, you'll know about it already. I definitely fall into that camp. I was in a restaurant once, on a romantic date, and asked for my meal to be served hot (as in warm temperature). About 10 seconds after eating it, I was overwhelmed by a terrible feeling of heat. Welts erupted all over my mouth, tears rolled down my cheeks and I was burning up everywhere. It turned out they'd put lots of hot chillies in my dish, thinking I meant a different type of 'hot'.

Getting organized

57

MENU PLAN

Now you know my Ten Steps to Get it Together, here's an example of a typical menu plan I'd recommend to a client, along with a handy shopping list. It will take a while to get your storecupboard fully stocked, but simply add a few ingredients each week. You might want to use this plan to get started, or feel free to create your own and dive straight into the recipe section.

Saturday:
Shopping List
» Herbal teas: nettle, mint, camomile
» Staples: mung beans, kidney beans, olive oil, wheat-free pasta, millet, brown rice
» Oils: olive
» Flavourings: vegetable bouillon powder (or ingredients for Vegetable Stock on p.222), miso soup sachets, nutmeg, root ginger, tamari sauce, bay leaves, turmeric, cumin
» Fruit: lemons, apples, mango, bananas, pineapple, blueberries, strawberries, pears
» Vegetables: onions, garlic, carrots, spinach, celery, black olives (pitted), pumpkin (or squash), asparagus, sweet potatoes, cabbage, green beans, avocados, cucumber, rocket (or watercress), baby gem lettuce, endive, radishes, red/yellow pepper, spring onions, beansprouts, leeks, parsnip, marinated artichokes, cherry tomatoes, baby spinach, shiitake mushrooms
» Fresh herbs: parsley, coriander, thyme, rosemary, basil
» Nuts: almonds, pine nuts, Brazil nuts, chestnuts
» Seeds: hemp, sunflower, pumpkin
» Milks: soya
» Protein: chicken breasts, salmon fillets, smoked tofu, goat's cheese

Sunday Evening:

» Make two batches of soup; Carrot & Almond (p.96) and Spinach (p.104). Transfer into airtight containers and keep in the fridge.

Monday

» On waking: Cup of warm water with squeeze fresh lemon juice
» Breakfast: Pineapple Prize Smoothie (p.76)
» Lunch: Carrot & Almond Soup (p.96), Green Salad (p.128)
» Dinner: Baked Salmon (p.147), add a small fillet for tomorrow's lunch
» Snacks: Whole pepper, pumpkin and sunflower seeds
» Drinks: 2 litres still mineral water and various herbal teas or vegetable juices

Tuesday

» On waking: Cup of warm water with squeeze fresh lemon juice
» Breakfast: Veggie Virgin Juice (p.67)
» Lunch: Carrot & Almond Soup (p.96), Baked Salmon (p.147) with baby gem lettuce
» Dinner: Lettuce and Cashew Nut Wraps (p.144) with Gourmet Brown Rice (p.185), make extra filling for tomorrow's lunch
» Snacks: Toasted Nori Strips (p.209), berries
» Drinks: 2 litres still mineral water and various herbal teas or vegetable juices

Wednesday

» On waking: Cup of warm water with squeeze fresh lemon juice

» Breakfast: Cinnamon Millet Porridge (p.90)

» Lunch: Spinach Soup (p.104), Lettuce and Cashew Nut Wraps (p.144)

» Dinner: Baked Butterflied Chicken with Shiitake Mushrooms (p.141), make extra for tomorrow's lunch, and Crunchy Kale (p.196)

» Snacks: Small punnet blueberries, rice cakes with Guacamole Dip (p.203)

» Drinks: 2 litres still mineral water and various herbal teas or vegetable juices

Thursday

» On waking: Cup of warm water with squeeze fresh lemon juice

» Breakfast: Fruit Salad (p.86)

» Lunch: Spinach Soup (p.104), Baked Butterflied Chicken with Shiitake Mushrooms (p.141)

» Dinner: Mung Bean Casserole (p.177), make extra and freeze

» Snacks: Brazil nuts, dates

» Drinks: 2 litres still mineral water and various herbal teas or vegetable juices

Friday

» On waking: Cup of warm water with squeeze fresh lemon juice

» Breakfast: Ginger Zinger (p.69)

» Lunch: Miso Soup (made from sachet), Mung Bean Casserole (p.177)

» Dinner: Stuffed Courgettes (p.185)

- » Snacks: Sunflower seeds, Black Olive Tapenade (p.203) with vegetable crudités
- » Drinks: 2 litres still mineral water and various herbal teas or vegetable juices

Saturday
- » On waking: Cup of warm water with squeeze fresh lemon juice
- » Breakfast: Mango Mania (p.75)
- » Lunch: Best Ever Beetroot Soup (p.99), Warm Chicken Salad (p.123)
- » Dinner: Smoked Tofu and Bean Burger (p.155) with Sweet Potato Wedges (p.206) and Crunchy Kale (p.196)
- » Snacks: Brazil nuts, grapes
- » Drinks: 2 litres still mineral water and various herbal teas or vegetable juices

Sunday
- » On waking: Cup of warm water with squeeze fresh lemon juice
- » Breakfast: Apple Action (p.80)
- » Lunch: Chestnut Roast (p.152) served with lightly steamed cabbage
- » Dinner: Hemp Pumpkin Soup (p.100)
- » Snacks: Baked Apple (p.216), not straight after lunch
- » Drinks: 2 litres still mineral water and various herbal teas or vegetable juices

Extra options for vegetarians
- » Dr Gillian's Shepherdess Pie (p.143)
- » Mediterranean Black-Eye Pea Casserole (p.146)
- » Aubergine and Chickpea Tagine (p.160)
- » Stir-Fry Vegetables with Arame (p.193)

FOUR
JUICES &
SMOOTHIES

Here's my biggest tip so far. Whenever you feel blue, toxic, unwell, or just plain tired, there's no better remedy than a glass of freshly made fruit or vegetable juices. It's a sure-fire way of injecting a cocktail of the most active health-giving compounds into your body.

JUICE JAMBOREE

I'd like you to get into the habit of drinking three to four glasses of fresh juices a week (or at least at weekends) right now – before you get to the point of no return. Vegetable juices are even healthier than fruit, but whichever you go for, make sure you use organic produce. You will need a juicer for most of the juices in this chapter – if you have a food processor or liquidizer but don't have a juicer yet then feel free to start with the smoothie recipes (pp.74–81) and then progress to juices.

TO PEEL OR NOT TO PEEL?

When you buy organic, there's no need to ever peel, so think how much time you will save. I'm also a great advocate of leaving on the skin for its nutritional and energetic benefits – and this can apply even when the fruit and veg are juiced, so make sure you leave it on before putting them through the juicer. Whether you buy organic or non-organic, wash and scrub the skin thoroughly, and for non-organic fruit and vegetables it is best to peel.

The juice recipes in this section are just some examples of what you can do. But be creative and try out as many combinations as you like. The sky's the limit!

FRUIT JUICES

Most of you will already be used to the concept of juicing fresh fruits. Use the recipes below as a starting point, choosing familiar varieties at first, then go for more exotic choices when you're ready. For each recipe, just push the fruits through the juicer nozzle, then pour into a tall glass and serve.

Pure pear

A simple one this, just made from pears. Steep a few fresh mint leaves in it before drinking – it will add to the colour and flavour, and will help your digestion!

SERVES 1–2
4 ripe pears, roughly chopped

Caribbean cooler

SERVES 1–2
half a pineapple
1 papaya, deseeded

Top Tip
Pineapple is a good source of vitamin C, which is great for your immune system and may help protect against colds.

Juices and smoothies

Bountiful berries

SERVES 1–2
1 punnet strawberries, hulled
half-punnet raspberries
2 apples, roughly chopped

Total cleanser

Another really easy one, you can either put the grapefruit
through a juicer or use a citrus press.

SERVES 1–2
2 whole red grapefruits, roughly chopped or halved

Winter warmer

SERVES 1–2
4 apples, roughly chopped
sprinkles of cinnamon to garnish

VEGETABLE JUICES

Vegetable juices are even healthier than fruit juices. They
are my own particular preference, but they can be an acquired
taste. It is a taste that can be enjoyed, however – it's simply
a case of retraining your taste buds. After all, if we can enjoy
the unnatural chemicalized flavours of soda pops and beers
– which, frankly, don't taste that good initially – then we can
certainly learn to love natural pure juices that come from
the earth. When I was a student, I remember having friends
who actually had to teach themselves how to like beer just
to stay in with the crowd. The fact is that vegetable juices,
once you're used to them, are delicious – and have side-effects
that can only be positive and beneficial to your health.

If you're new to vegetable juices and feel a bit
apprehensive about drinking them, start off with this one:

VEGGIE VIRGIN JUICE FOR FIRST-TIMERS

Juice enough carrots to fill half a 250-ml glass. Then fill the
other half of the glass with fresh apple juice. In other words,
it's 50 per cent carrots and 50 per cent apple. Drink it for the
first two weeks of your juice journey. After that, start to
reduce the percentage of apple juice and either increase the
amount of carrot or, preferably, add some juiced celery and
juiced cucumbers. Before long, you'll find you're becoming
a real vegetable juice junkie.

My aim is to get you to the stage where you are drinking
vegetable juices without the apple or fruit juices mixed in.
But don't fret over this. Just do your best until it feels right
and feel free to experiment with all kinds of variations and
creations of your own, always bearing in mind that adding
carrot juice will make your veggie juices taste sweeter
(and apple juice sweeter still). Even when you get used

to drinking veggie juices on their own, you may find they make you feel nauseous if you drink them first thing in the morning. If you fall into this category, start off with fruit juices in the mornings then continue with vegetable juices for the rest of the day.

Veggie vitality

This juice is so nutrient-dense that I even make it for my clients. The recipe below is merely supposed to be a guideline – you may have to experiment with the proportions to get the taste you want. If you want more of a neutral taste, then add more cucumber; if you want it sweeter, add more carrots or peppers.

SERVES 1–2
8 tomatoes, roughly chopped
7 carrots, trimmed
2 celery stalks, trimmed
half a cucumber, halved lengthways
1 handful cabbage leaves, roughly chopped
half a yellow pepper, deseeded and roughly chopped
2 green beans or snow peas
1 garlic clove, peeled
half an onion, peeled

Cool as a cucumber

This is a great skin revitalizer! It's also one of the easiest juices to make because cucumbers have a very high water content, which makes them naturals for juicing.

SERVES 1–2
1 cucumber, halved lengthways
2 celery stalks, trimmed
1-cm piece fresh root ginger (optional)

Sprout surprise

SERVES 1–2
1 handful alfalfa sprouts
1 apple, roughly chopped
5 carrots, trimmed

Ginger zinger

This is a terrific breakfast juice that will perk up your whole system.

SERVES 1–2
2 apples, roughly chopped
2 ripe pears, roughly chopped
1-cm piece fresh root ginger

A note about ginger
You'll see that I've normally specified a 1-cm piece of root ginger, but add as much as you like, according to taste.

Wake-up

SERVES 1–2
6 carrots, trimmed
1–2 apples, roughly chopped
1-cm piece fresh root ginger

Top tip
Raw garlic in a juice is fantastic for helping to keep blood pressure in check.

Happy tummy

This is a cool, refreshing stomach-easer. Adding the non-bitter aloe (available from a health food shop) will really help soothe the gut and help digestion.

SERVES 1–2
2 apples, roughly chopped
1 lemon, skin and rind removed and halved
1 handful fresh mint
2 tbsp non-bitter aloe vera juice (optional)

Antibacterial and immunity booster

If you find the taste of this too sharp, add some celery or cucumber to neutralize the taste.

SERVES 1–2
1 handful broccoli sprouts, clover sprouts or alfalfa sprouts
1 floret fresh broccoli
1 small radish
2 carrots, trimmed
1 garlic clove, peeled, or 1 tsp chopped red onion

Relaxer

SERVES 1–2
1 cucumber, halved lengthways
2 celery stalks, trimmed
3 lettuce leaves, roughly chopped

Beetroot bliss for the liver

Perfect for boosting flagging energy levels.

SERVES 1-2
3 carrots, trimmed
3 celery sticks, trimmed
half a cucumber, halved lengthways
1 small beetroot, roughly chopped

Mineral mania

This juice can sometimes seem bitter on first tasting. The first few times you make it, feel free to add some apple juice to taste. For a real protein boost and even more minerals, add some liquid Wild Blue Green Algae.

SERVES 1-2
3 kale leaves, roughly chopped
2 fresh parsley sprigs
4 carrots, trimmed

Fennel fun

SERVES 1-2
half a beetroot
4 carrots, trimmed
4 celery sticks, trimmed
1 fennel, quartered lengthways

VEGGIE FACTS

» **Asparagus: Support for the kidneys** The alkaloid asparagine, found in asparagus (and also in potatoes and beetroot), stimulates the kidneys and has a strong diuretic effect.

» **Avocado (vegetable fruit): Heart protector** An excellent source of oleic acid, which is great for cardiovascular health. Also rich in vitamin E, which is essential for healthy skin.

» **Beans and mangetout: Protectors against diabetes** Pod vegetables are absorbed slowly and can help control insulin and reduce the risk of insulin resistance/diabetes.

» **Beansprouts: Nutritional superstars** Beansprouts are high in many minerals and vitamins that boost health and immunity.

» **Beetroot: Strength- and blood-builder** Very rich in immune-boosting betacarotene and folate.

» **Broccoli: Cancer protection** Broccoli contains phytochemicals with significant anti-cancer effects.

» **Cabbage: Colon cancer protection** A rich vegetable source of vitamin C and a sulphur-containing compound called sinigrin that has excellent colon cancer fighting properties.

» **Carrot: Good for skin and eyes** Rich in betacarotene which is good for the immune system as well as for skin and eye health.

» **Celery: Cholesterol and blood pressure regulator** Celery contains active compounds called pthalides, which relax the muscles of the arteries that regulate blood pressure. It also has calming and diuretic properties.

» **Cress: Protector against cancer** Member of the brassica (cruciferous veg) family, with the same anti-cancer health benefits.

- » **Cucumber: Heart protector** A strong diuretic, it can also help to lower blood pressure.
- » **Dandelion leaves: Useful for arthritis**
  They help balance acid/alkaline levels in the body, which makes them useful in arthritic conditions.
- » **Fennel: Irritable Bowel Syndrome relief** As a very good source of fibre, the fennel bulb may help to reduce elevated cholesterol levels as well as the diarrhoea or constipation symptomatic of irritable bowel syndrome.
- » **Onion: Immunity-booster** Whether you have a cold or the flu, onions have amazing immune-boosting qualities. They are also antibacterial and antiseptic. (Leeks have similar but milder actions.)
- » **Peppers: Immunity-boosters** One of the richest sources of vitamin C, peppers provide support for the immune system. Yellow, red and orange peppers also contain high levels of the antioxidant betacarotene.
- » **Tomato: Powerful antioxidant** A rich source of lycopene, which has strong antioxidant, anti-cancer, anti-ageing properties.
- » **Watercress: Good for bone health** An excellent source of magnesium and calcium for strong bones and hormonal balance. Watercress is also a good source of iron – to help beat fatigue – and sulphur, which is good for hair and nails.

SMOOTHIES

Blended fruit is a terrific energizer and cleanser and I love its taste and texture. In fact, I usually start my day with a fruit smoothie. When filming *You Are What You Eat*, I often have to leave home very early in the morning, so when I get up I have a cup of warm water and then make my smoothie. I make loads and put it all into tumbler containers which I take with me. You never know, you may well have seen me sitting on a train tucking into my nutrient-laden fruit delicacies.

I use my smoothies as a delivery medium for superfoods and added herbs. I think of them as vitamin infusions, or what I sometimes call my 'nutrient shot'. Here's my list of the key superfoods you can add to any of the smoothie recipes in this section.

Key superfoods

» Barley grass powder
» Bee pollen granules
» Chlorella powder
» Dr Gillian McKeith's Living Food Energy Powder
» Flax seeds
» Liquid algae (the most easy-to-digest form of vegetable protein and a powerhouse of mineral nutrients)
» Non-bitter aloe liquid
» Spirulina powder
» Wheatgrass powder
» Wild blue green algae

Top tip

If you want your smoothies to be less thick then simply add some water.

All these superfoods should be available at your local health food shop. Don't use all of them at once. Just pick one or two and use them in your smoothies for one particular day, week or month and simply follow the instructions on the label for how much to use. When you've used the bottle(s) up, go out and get something else on the list. It's good to change your superfoods every now and again.

Smoothies are really easy to make. You can make them thick or thin, as you like – the thicker the smoothie, the more filling it will be. Practice makes perfect. Play around with all kinds of combinations and find out what you like.

Mango mania

This is my Number One top favourite smoothie. It's very filling, tastes heavenly – and it's a great way to get your bowels going.

SERVES 1-2
1 large mango, peeled, stoned and roughly chopped
2 bananas, peeled and roughly chopped
Choice of superfood (see p.74)
1 handful each of blueberries and raspberries, to serve

Blend the mango, banana and choice of superfood until smooth and creamy. Put the blueberries and raspberries in a tall glass, reserving a few raspberries. Pour the smoothie over the berries and serve garnished with the reserved raspberries.

For a change ...
Try Warmed Mango Mania, as a variation. Using the same ingredients as above, warm the mango and bananas in a pot with some water. Place the mixture in a blender, add your choice of superfood and blend. Pour over the raw berries or some chopped apples. Perfect for the cold months, or if you need warming up!

Pineapple prize

SERVES 1–2
2 bananas, peeled and roughly chopped
1 mango, peeled, stoned and roughly chopped
half a pineapple, peeled and chopped

Blend until smooth and creamy. Add your favourite superfood for extra nutritional benefits!

Berry blaster

SERVES 1–2
1 large or 2 small bananas, peeled and roughly chopped
1 handful blueberries, to serve

Blend the bananas until smooth and creamy. Put the blueberries in a tall glass. Pour the smoothie over the berries and serve.

Very berry blast-off

SERVES 1–2
2 handfuls strawberries, hulled
2 handfuls raspberries
2 apples, cored and roughly chopped
120 ml non-bitter aloe or water (to blend the apple).
1 tsp liquid algae
1 handful blueberries, to serve

Blend the berries, apples and liquid algae until smooth and creamy. Put the blueberries in a tall glass. Pour the smoothie over the berries and serve.

Top tip
Warm or stew apples in the winter – then you won't have to add water to make them blend easily.

Sexy starter

SERVES 1–2

1 handful of strawberries, hulled
1 handful of blueberries
1 handful of raspberries
1 large banana, peeled and roughly chopped

Blend until smooth and creamy then serve.

Peach medley

SERVES 1–2

4 peaches, stoned and quartered
2 ripe pears, cored and roughly chopped
1 apple, cored and roughly chopped

Add 120 ml water. Blend until smooth and creamy then serve.

Mineral mover

SERVES 1–2

3 ripe pears, cored and roughly chopped
2 apples, cored and roughly chopped (slightly warmed
so they will blend easily)
3 apricots, stoned
1 tsp liquid algae

Blend until smooth and creamy then serve.

Berry beauty

SERVES 1-2
2 handfuls strawberries, hulled
1 large or 2 small mangoes, peeled, stoned and roughly chopped

Blend until smooth and creamy then serve.

Vitamin C cocktail

You haven't lived till you've tasted this one!

SERVES 1-2
1 pineapple, peeled and roughly chopped
2 handfuls strawberries, hulled
1 handful gooseberries, blueberries or raspberries, to serve

Blend the pineapple chunks and strawberries until smooth and creamy. Put your choice of berries in a tall glass. Pour the smoothie over the berries and serve.

Pear perfection

SERVES 1-2
6 ripe pears, cored and roughly chopped
2 bananas, peeled and roughly chopped

Blend until smooth and creamy then serve. Add a little water if the mixture is too thick.

Kiwi cooler

SERVES 1
2 kiwi fruit
1 apple or pear, cored and roughly chopped

Blend until smooth and creamy then serve. Add a little
water if the mixture is too thick.

Pineapple puree

SERVES 1–2
1 pineapple, peeled and roughly chopped
2 small bananas, peeled and roughly chopped
1 peach, stoned and chopped, to serve

Blend the pineapple and bananas until smooth and creamy.
Put the chopped peach in a tall glass. Pour the smoothie
over the peach and serve.

Fruit frenzy

SERVES 1–2
3 peaches, stoned and quartered
3 ripe pears, cored and roughly chopped
3 plums, stoned
1 handful raspberries, blackberries, or other berries
of your choice, to serve

Blend the peaches, pears and plums until smooth and
creamy. Put the berries in a tall glass. Pour the smoothie
over the berries and serve.

Yum-yum delight

Kids can make smoothies too. This one was invented by my wee daughter. I love it – and so do my clients.

SERVES 1–2
2 plums, stoned
2 nectarines, stoned and quartered
2 ripe pears, cored and roughly chopped
half a handful of blueberries
12 strawberries, hulled

Add 120 ml water. Blend until smooth and creamy then serve.

Apple action

Another kids' invention – inspired by my other (even wee-er) daughter.

SERVES 1–2
2 apples, cored and roughly chopped
3 ripe pears, cored and roughly chopped
1 handful strawberries, hulled and chopped (optional)

Add 120 ml water. Blend until smooth and creamy.
Garnish with chopped-up strawberries if desired.

Pear and strawberry smoothie

SERVES 1–2
2 ripe pears, cored and roughly chopped
250 g strawberries, hulled

Blend until smooth and creamy then serve.

Juicy smoothie

This is a fantastic, filling juice-smoothie combination – great
for detox days! It's absolutely delicious – and full of essential
'thinny' fats.

SERVES 1–2

6 carrots, trimmed
1 apple, cored and roughly chopped
1 soft avocado, peeled, stoned and roughly chopped
10 basil leaves
1 lemon wedge

Push the carrots and apple through a juicer. Blend the
juice with the avocado and basil leaves. Squeeze a dash
of lemon into the smoothie and serve.

FRUIT FACTS

» **Apple: Cholesterol-buster** Their pectin content may
lower cholesterol.

» **Apricot: Sight-saver** Their vitamin A content promotes
good vision.

» **Banana: Great de-stressor** Rich in mineral potassium,
they're fantastic for destressing and lowering high blood
pressure.

» **Blueberry: The sexy superfruit** A good source of zinc
and other antioxidants and nutrients associated with
sex hormones in men and women.

» **Cantaloupe melon: Lung-saver** Betacarotene and
vitamin C content in cantaloupe melons could be life-savers
if you're exposed to passive smoking.

» **Cherry: Nature's joint rescuer** Cherries may help a wide
range of conditions affecting the joints, including arthritis,
gout and rheumatism.

» **Cranberry: Good for urinary tract infections** Their unique anti-bacterial action helps to maintain urinary tract health.

» **Date: Blood-builder** Dates are high in potassium and dietary fibre. They are also a good source of energy-boosting iron.

» **Fig: Bone-strengthener** Figs are a fruit source of calcium, a mineral that has many functions, including promoting bone density.

» **Grape: Blood-purifier** Grapes contain ingredients that may help to purify your glands and blood.

» **Grapefruit: Antibacterial detoxer** Phytochemicals and antioxidants in grapefruit help fight disease and infection.

» **Kiwi fruit: Heart-helper** Kiwi fruit is an excellent source of nutrients that protect the blood vessels and heart.

» **Lemon and lime: Good blood building** Their high vitamin C content helps iron absorption. They're great gas-busters too.

» **Mango: Immune-booster** Vitamin C powerhouses with impressive levels of disease-fighting carotenoids, vitamin A, folate, potassium and fibre.

» **Papaya: Colon-helper** The nutrients and fibre in papaya have also been shown to be helpful in the prevention of colon cancer.

» **Peach: Nature's anti-cold remedy** A good source of vitamin C, which is vital for the proper function of a healthy immune system.

» **Pear: Age-fighter** A great source of vitamin C and copper – both antioxidant nutrients that help protect cells in the body from oxygen-related damage caused by free radicals.

» **Pineapple: Energy-booster** An excellent source of manganese, thiamin and riboflavin, which are important for energy production.

» **Plum: Digestive aid** Rich in bromelain, a sulphur-containing group of enzymes that can aid the digestion of proteins.

» **Prune: Appetite-suppressant** The soluble fibre in prunes promotes a sense of satisfied fullness after eating by slowing down the rate at which food leaves the stomach. So prunes can also help prevent overeating and weight gain.

» **Raisin: Bone-builder** A top source of boron – a mineral that is critical for bone health and the prevention of osteoporosis (bone softening).

» **Raspberry: Brain food** Antioxidant phytonutrients in raspberries can help improve learning capacity and motor skills.

» **Strawberry: Anti-cancer compounds** The ellagitannin content of strawberries has been associated with helping to prevent cancer.

» **Watermelon: Anti-inflammatory** They contain nutrients that can help quench the inflammation that contributes to conditions such as asthma, diabetes, colon cancer, and arthritis.

FIVE
BREAKFASTS

I always say that you should breakfast like a king. When you wake up in the morning, you have in effect been fasting for several hours. The body is in need of food and digestive energy is at its strongest. When you eat a proper breakfast, it is like giving yourself an energy injection and there are now strong, credible studies which show the benefits of eating a healthy breakfast: including weight loss, enhancing memory and improving brain function.

Personally, I used to find that if I ever missed breakfast I would suffer from headaches and mid-morning energy slumps. Now my favourite way to start the day is either with a smoothie (pp.74–81) or porridge (pp.88–91). You can even have soup for breakfast (p.88), and on the weekend you might want to indulge in a frittata (p.92) or homemade beans on toast (p.93).

Fruit simpling

This simply means eating one single fruit for maximum ease of digestion. Remember to wash all fruit. Your raw fruit of choice might be any one of the following:

SERVES 1
1 whole pineapple
1 whole papaya
1 whole mango
2 whole apples
A bunch of grapes, red or white
A bowl of blueberries, strawberries or raspberries

Autumn fruit salad

SERVES 4
KEEPS FOR TWO DAYS IN THE FRIDGE
4 apples, quartered, cored and chopped
4 ripe pears, quartered, cored and sliced
8 plums, halved, stoned and sliced
250 ml freshly pressed apple juice

Combine the ingredients together and serve immediately.

Fruit salad with warm pear sauce

SERVES 4
KEEPS FOR TWO DAYS IN THE FRIDGE
4 ripe pears, cored and chopped
2 tbsp lemon juice
300 g strawberries, hulled
300 g raspberries
300 g blueberries

1. Place the pears in a small saucepan with the lemon juice. Add enough water to cover. Bring to the boil, reduce heat and cook gently over a low heat until quite soft. Remove from liquid and allow to cool. Blend in a food processor or with a hand-held blender until smooth. Add a little water if you prefer the sauce to be thinner.

2. Mix the berries together in a bowl and pour over the pear sauce. Serve immediately or chill until required.

Muesli

The key when developing your own muesli recipe is not to mix too many different ingredients. Keep it simple. See below for ingredient ideas. If you are food combining then don't include any fruit in your muesli (see p.18).

GRAIN
Barley flakes
Buckwheat
Millet flakes
Oat bran
Puffed corn
Puffed millet
Puffed rice
Rice bran
Rice flakes
Rolled barley
Rolled oats
Rolled rice
Rolled rye
Rolled wheat
Soy grits
Wheat bran
Wheatgerm

FRUIT
Apples
Apricots
Bananas
Blackberries
Blueberries
Currants
Dates
Dried paw paw
Dry papaya
Figs
Kiwi fruit
Peaches
Pears
Plums
Prunes
Raisins
Raspberries
Strawberries

SEEDS
Alfalfa seeds
Flax seeds
Hemp seeds (shelled)
Linseeds
Poppy seeds
Sesame seeds
Sunflower seeds

NUTS
Almonds
Brazil nuts
Cashews
Coconut
Hazelnuts
Macadamias
Peanuts (unsalted)
Walnuts

OTHER
Apple juice (freshly pressed)
Barley malt syrup
Cinnamon
Rice milk
Soya milk
Spelt milk

Miso barley soup

SERVES 1
4 tbsp pearl barley, presoaked for 12 hours
or overnight in cold water
1 packet instant miso soup

1. Drain the barley.
2. Bring 125 ml water to the boil, add the barley and bring back to boil. Lower the heat and simmer for 10–15 minutes.
3. Add the packet of soup. Stir and serve.

Breakfast soup blitz

This is one that I make all the time because it's so quick and easy.

SERVES 1–2
4 tbsp shiro miso
2 sachets white miso
2 red onions, peeled and diced
half a leek, washed, trimmed and finely sliced
200 g tofu, finely diced
half a fennel bulb, trimmed and finely sliced
250g curly kale, roughly chopped

1. Bring 250 ml water to the boil. Add the shiro miso and the white miso, lower the heat and simmer for 2 minutes.
2. Add all the other ingredients, stir, then turn off the heat and allow to stand for 8 minutes before serving.

Quinoa porridge

Quinoa comes in two forms: flakes and grain. I like the
texture and flavour of the grain best – it takes a wee bit
longer to cook, though we are only talking a matter of
minutes. See what you like best, so try both. And of course,
the flakes are super-quick if you are in a rush. Soya or rice
milk may be used as an alternative to the apple juice for
a creamier texture.

SERVES 2–4
250 g quinoa grains
quarter of a cinnamon stick
125 ml freshly pressed apple juice

1. Place the quinoa, cinnamon, apple juice and 325 ml water
in a medium-sized saucepan. Bring to the boil, then lower
the heat and simmer for 7–10 minutes, or until grains are
translucent.
2. Turn off the heat and allow to stand for 15 minutes before
serving. Delicious!

Vanilla barley porridge

SERVES 2–4
250 g barley groats, presoaked in water overnight
half a vanilla pod
2 tsp flax seeds

1. Drain the barley.
2. Place the barley in a medium to large saucepan along
with the vanilla pod and 1.5 litres water. Bring to the boil,
then lower the heat and simmer for 15 minutes.
3. Serve warm, sprinkled with flax seeds.

Cinnamon millet porridge

SERVES 2–4

250 g millet
1 cinnamon stick
zest of half a lemon
2 tbsp shelled hemp seeds

1. Place the millet, cinnamon and lemon zest, together with 1.25 litres water in a medium-sized pan and bring to the boil. Lower the heat, simmer for 1 hour.
2. Serve warm with the hemp seeds sprinkled on top.

Buckwheat, lemon and ginger porridge

SERVES 2–4

250 g buckwheat groats
juice and zest of 1 lemon
2-cm piece fresh root ginger, peeled and grated
1 pinch dried mixed herbal seasoning
1 handful of shelled hemp seeds

1. Place the buckwheat, lemon juice and zest, ginger, herbal seasoning and 1 litre water in a medium-sized pan. Bring to the boil, then lower the heat and simmer for 20 minutes.
2. Top with the hemp seeds and serve immediately.

Bran porridge

Hemp seeds contain the most perfect ratio of omega-3, omega-6 and omega-9, the good essential fatty acids for energy, glowing skin, lustrous hair and balanced hormones. And they taste great too.

SERVES 2–4
250 g mixed oat bran, oat groats and porridge oats
2 tbsp shelled hemp seeds
1 dessertspoonful malt barley syrup (optional)

1. Place the grains and 1.5 litres water (or rice milk for extra flavour) in a medium-sized saucepan. Bring to the boil, then lower the heat and simmer, stirring regularly, until thickened.
2. Turn off the heat and allow to stand for a few minutes. Before serving sprinkle some raw hemp seeds on top and drizzle over the malt barley syrup, if using.

Note about porridge
The simplest porridge to make is porridge oats with soya, millet, amaranth, spelt or rice milk. Simply combine 250 g porridge oats with 125 ml grain milk in a pan, bring to the boil then lower the heat and simmer for 15–20 minutes. Oats are a great source of fibre and complex carbohydrates, good for sustained energy. A diet high in natural fibre and low in processed foods can also be beneficial for heart health.

Frittata with cherry tomatoes and baby spinach

I do not advocate the over-eating of eggs but as a special treat try this recipe now and again.

SERVES 2–3
6 organic eggs
1 tsp olive oil
200 g cherry tomatoes,
cut in half
350 g baby spinach
chopped fresh basil
chopped fresh parsley

1. Preheat the oven to 200C/gas mark 6.

2. Whisk the eggs with 2 tablespoons of water.

3. Heat the oil in a cast-iron pan or frittata plate with 1 tablespoon of water. Add the tomatoes and spinach and cook until the spinach begins to wilt. Sprinkle over the herbs.

4. Pour in the eggs and transfer to the preheated oven.

5. Bake for 10–12 minutes until well-risen and golden brown.

6. Slice in wedges and serve with a side salad.

Grilled peaches

SERVES 4
4 ripe peaches, halved and stoned
200 g strawberries, hulled and halved
200 g blueberries

1. Preheat the grill on its highest setting.

2. Place the peaches cut side up on the grill pan.

3. Cook for 3–4 minutes or until lightly grilled.

4. Transfer to 4 plates, top with the fresh berries and serve.

Home-made beans on squash bread toast

SERVES 4
400-g can organic tomatoes
410-g can haricot beans
4 slices Squash Bread (see p.207)
1 tsp chopped fresh oregano

1. Place the tomatoes in a small pan and bring to the boil. Lower the heat and simmer for 20 minutes, breaking up the tomatoes as they cook. Add the beans and cook for a further 5 minutes.

2. Toast the bread, top with the beans mixture and serve garnished with the fresh oregano.

SIX
SOUPS

You'll find each soup in this chapter fantastic for you in different ways. Try all the recipes out, but also think about using them as a guide to creating variations that you like. Be adventurous with flavourings – adding herbs at the end of cooking can make a huge difference.

Get creative with seeds too. Use hemp, flax, amaranth or poppy seeds. They're not only delicious and flavoursome, but packed with minerals and essential fatty acids that are crucial for weight management, energy and optimum digestion.

Carrot and almond soup

Carrots are a source of anti-ageing antioxidants, while almonds are a powerhouse of nutrients, incuding magnesium, which is important for supporting adrenal function. Low levels of magnesium have been associated with nervous tension, so almonds are a natural stress-buster.

SERVES 4
2 onions, peeled and chopped
2 garlic cloves, peeled and chopped
6 carrots, trimmed, peeled and sliced
2 celery stalks, trimmed and chopped
1 tbsp wheat-free vegetable bouillon powder
2–3 tbsp chopped fresh coriander, stalks reserved
2–3 tbsp chopped fresh parsley, stalks reserved
100 g ground almonds

1. Place the onions, garlic, carrots and celery in a large saucepan. Add 1.25 litres boiling water and the bouillon powder. Bring to the boil and add the herb stalks.
2. Lower the heat and simmer for 30 minutes until vegetables are tender when pierced with a knife.
3. Remove from the heat and allow to cool slightly. Strain, reserving the stock. Remove the herb stalks, then blend the vegetables in a food processor or with a hand-held blender until smooth.
4. Return the mixture to the pan and add the ground almonds and enough of the reserved stock to make a soup-like consistency.
5. Reheat, then divide between warmed soup bowls and serve garnished with chopped fresh coriander and parsley.

For a change ...

This soup is also very good made with sweet potatoes. Just add one sweet potato, peeled and diced, in place of two of the carrots and cook as above.

Creamy broccoli soup

Broccoli is a friend to your liver. It contains a compound called sulphorophane, which has been shown to inhibit the growth of free radicals, those nasty molecules that age us and make us feel tired.

SERVES 4
1 fennel bulb, trimmed and finely diced
1 wheat-free vegetable stock cube
3 whole heads broccoli, cut into florets and stems finely sliced
1 handful fresh tarragon
1 handful fresh sage
1 punnet alfalfa sprouts (or any other sprouted seeds of choice)

1. Bring a medium-sized pan of water to the boil, then add the fennel and stock cube. Lower the heat and simmer for 5–7 minutes. Add the broccoli, including the stems, and simmer for a further 4–5 minutes.
2. Remove from the heat and add the tarragon and sage. Allow to cool then blend the soup in a food processor or with a hand-held blender until smooth.
3. Divide between warmed soup bowls. Sprinkle with the sprouts and serve immediately.

Turnip and leek soup

A firm favourite in our house. Leeks belong to the same family of vegetable as onions and garlic and contain many of the same beneficial nutrients. They are also a good source of manganese, vitamin B6, vitamin C, folate and iron. This combination makes leeks helpful in stabilizing blood sugar, helping to slow the absorption of sugars from the intestinal tract and ensure that they are properly metabolized in the body.

SERVES 4
1 turnip, trimmed, peeled and diced
1 wheat-free vegetable stock cube
1 tbsp wheat-free vegetable bouillon powder
6 celery stalks, trimmed and roughly chopped
6 leeks, washed, trimmed and chopped
3 small onions, peeled and chopped
4 tbsp chopped fresh tarragon

1. Place 750 ml water in a large saucepan, bring to the boil and add the turnip, stock cube and bouillon powder. Lower the heat and simmer for 10 minutes.

2. Add the celery, leeks and onions and simmer for a further 15 minutes.

3. Remove from the heat and allow to cool, add the tarragon, then blend in a food processor or with a hand-held blender to your desired consistency.

4. Reheat, divide between warmed soup bowls and serve.

Best-ever beetroot soup

If you are tired, this is the soup for you. Go to a mirror,
pull down your lower eyelid and check to see the colour of
your inner inside lid. If it's pale, you may need more iron.
And of course, you need my best-ever soup.

SERVES 4
1 tbsp olive oil
1 onion, peeled and chopped
1 garlic clove, peeled and chopped
2 celery stalks, trimmed and sliced
1 large parsnip, trimmed, peeled and grated
6 small raw beetroot, trimmed, peeled and grated
1 wheat-free vegetable stock cube
1 tsp wheat-free vegetable bouillon powder
1 tbsp cider vinegar
1 sweet potato, peeled and diced
third of a cucumber, peeled and diced
2 tbsp finely chopped fresh dill

1. Place the oil, onion, garlic and celery in a large saucepan
with 3 tablespoons of water. Cook over a moderate to low
heat, stirring frequently, for 3–4 minutes, until soft but
not coloured.
2. Add the parsnip, beetroot, stock cube and bouillon
powder to the pan with 1.25 litres cold water. Bring to
the boil, then lower the heat and simmer for 30 minutes.
3. Stir in the vinegar and sweet potato and continue to
simmer for 10 minutes or until the vegetables are tender
when pierced with a knife.
4. Ladle into warmed soup bowls and serve garnished
with the diced cucumber mixed with the dill.

Hemp pumpkin soup

Pumpkin has a delicious sweet flavour. It helps to regulate sugar balance and is high in potassium and vitamin C, and its seeds contain zinc – a libido- and immune-system booster. Hemp seeds provide a perfect ratio of essential fatty acids, more so than any other seed.

SERVES 4

1 pumpkin or seasonal squash, peeled, deseeded and cut into 2.5-cm pieces
1 bunch asparagus, roughly chopped (tips reserved for a salad)
2 large sweet potatoes, peeled and cut into 2.5-cm pieces
3 carrots, trimmed, peeled and chopped
6 onions, peeled and roughly chopped
1 wheat-free vegetable stock cube
1 garlic clove, peeled and chopped
2 tbsp chopped fresh coriander
2 tbsp shelled hemp seeds
2 tbsp pumpkin seeds

1. Bring a large pan with 1 litre water to the boil then add the pumpkin or squash, asparagus, sweet potatoes, carrots, onions and stock cube. Bring back to the boil, then lower the heat and simmer for 10–15 minutes or until the vegetables are tender when pierced with a knife.
2. Remove from the heat and add the garlic and coriander.
3. Allow to cool and then blend in a food processor or with a hand-held blender to your desired consistency.
4. Reheat gently. Divide between warmed bowls and serve garnished with the seeds.

White bean and cabbage soup

SERVES 4

1 onion, peeled and finely sliced
2 celery stalks, trimmed and finely sliced
1 whole white cabbage, finely sliced
1 wheat-free vegetable stock cube
1 tbsp wheat-free vegetable bouillon powder
410-g can butter beans, drained and rinsed
2 tbsp chopped fresh parsley
4 tbsp fresh garden peas

1. Place the onion, celery, cabbage, stock cube and bouillon powder in a medium-sized pan with enough water to cover.
2. Bring to the boil, then lower the heat and simmer for 30–40 minutes, adding a little more water if necessary.
3. Add the butter beans and simmer for a further 10 minutes.
4. Divide between warmed soup bowls and serve immediately, garnished with the parsley and peas.

Butternut squash and sweet potato soup

The digestive dynamo of all soups. If you have a line down the middle of your tongue or teeth marks round the sides – it could be a sign of a weakened spleen and tummy – then this soup is for you. It will help you absorb more nutrients from all the foods you eat.

SERVES 4

1 butternut squash, peeled, deseeded and diced
1 sweet potato, peeled and diced
2 carrots, trimmed, peeled and sliced
1 fennel bulb, trimmed and chopped
6 shallots, peeled and finely sliced
1 wheat-free vegetable stock cube
1 garlic clove, peeled and chopped
4 tbsp chopped fresh parsley
1 bunch radishes, trimmed and chopped
4–6 tbsp pumpkin seeds (optional)

1. Bring a large pan half-filled with water to the boil. Add the squash, sweet potato, carrots, fennel, shallots and stock cube.

2. Bring to the boil, then lower the heat and simmer for 10–12 minutes.

3. Remove from the heat and add the garlic.

4. Allow to cool, then strain the vegetables into a large bowl to keep the stock.

5. Add half the stock to the vegetables and blend in a food processor or with a hand-held blender to desired consistency.

6. Reheat the soup gently, adding more of the reserved stock if necessary.

7. Divide between warmed soup bowls and serve garnished with the parsley, radishes and pumpkin seeds if using.

Ten-minute miso fish soup

This soup has been a true success with my TV participants because it is so easy to make and can be ready in 10 minutes. It is loaded with nutrients and miso is a tremendous source of good bacteria.

SERVES 4
1 garlic clove, peeled and thinly sliced
2.5-cm piece fresh root-ginger, peeled and finely sliced
1 packet instant miso soup
100 g skinless boned white fish, cut into chunks
8 mangetout, trimmed and sliced
1 red pepper, deseeded and chopped
1 pak choi, finely sliced
2 spring onions, trimmed and sliced
1 handful beansprouts
1 handful fresh garden peas

1. Bring 500 ml water to the boil in a medium-sized pan. Add the garlic, ginger and miso soup. Boil for 1 minute and then add the fish, mangetout and red pepper. Bring back to the boil and skim any foam that accumulates from the top with a slotted spoon. Cook for 2 minutes.
2. Add the pak choi and spring onions and cook for a further minute.
3. Divide between warmed soup bowls. Add the beansprouts and peas and serve immediately.

Spinach soup

If you are late in from work and are really starving here is a soup you can whip up in just a few minutes. Spinach contains good levels of vitamin B6, which helps lower levels of homocysteine in the body. High levels of homocysteine are associated with an increased risk of heart attack or stroke.

SERVES 4
1 onion, peeled and finely chopped
1 tsp olive oil
500 g fresh spinach
1 wheat-free vegetable stock cube
1 handful parsley stalks
fresh nutmeg, to taste
250 ml soya milk (optional)
1 tbsp pumpkin seeds
1 handful fresh baby spinach leaves

1. Place the onion, olive oil and 1 tablespoon of water in a large pan. Cook over a low to moderate heat for 2–3 minutes until soft.
2. Add the spinach, 500 ml boiling water, the stock cube and parsley stalks and cook for 5–7 minutes. Allow to cool slightly, then blend in a food processor or with a hand-held blender until smooth.
3. Return to the pan, season with a little nutmeg, stir in the soya milk (or 250 ml water or Vegetable Stock on p.222) and reheat gently.
4. Divide between warmed soup bowls and serve garnished with the pumpkin seeds and raw baby spinach leaves.

Super green kale soup

If you feel tired, irritable, constipated or crave sweet things then this is a great soup for you. Getting your fair share of dark green leafy vegetables is extremely important. Kale is an excellent source of vitamin C – just one cup contains nearly 90 per cent of the recommended daily intake. It also contains magnesium, which has been shown to help migraine sufferers.

SERVES 4
1 tbsp olive oil
1 large onion, peeled and sliced
1 garlic clove, peeled and crushed
2 turnips, trimmed, peeled and chopped
2 wheat-free vegetable stock cubes
2 courgettes, trimmed and sliced into 1-cm pieces
200 g curly kale, rinsed and drained
1 handful freshly chopped dill

1. Heat the oil in a large saucepan and gently cook the onion and garlic over a low to moderate heat for 4–5 minutes, stirring continuously to ensure the onion does not brown. Add the turnips and cook for a further 3 minutes.
2. Add 750 ml boiling water and the stock cubes. Bring to the boil, then lower the heat and simmer for 10 minutes.
3. Add the courgettes and kale and simmer for a further 5 minutes.
4. Allow to cool, then blend in a food processor or with a hand-held blender until smooth.
5. Divide between warmed soup bowls and serve garnished with dill.

Raw avocado and cucumber soup

Including as much raw food as possible in your food regime is essential. Avocado contains 14 minerals, including iron and potassium, and it also contains the all-important essential fatty acids. It's high on my list as a source of good fat.

SERVES 4
3 cucumbers, peeled
1 large ripe avocado, stoned, peeled and roughly chopped
juice of 1 lemon
1 garlic clove, peeled and chopped
3 tbsp chopped fresh mint leaves
1 red pepper, deseeded and finely chopped
1 yellow pepper, deseeded and finely chopped
1 tbsp finely sliced fresh chives

1. With an electric juicer, process two of the cucumbers into juice and reserve.
2. Roughly chop the remaining cucumber and blend with the avocado, lemon juice, garlic and mint in a food processor or with a hand-held blender until smooth. Add the reserved cucumber juice and blend again until mixed through.
3. Chill until required. Divide between cold soup bowls and serve garnished with the peppers and chives.

Tuscan bean soup

SERVES 4
2 onions, peeled and roughly chopped
2 tsp olive oil
2 celery stalks, trimmed and chopped
1 leek, washed, trimmed and finely chopped
6 garlic cloves, peeled and chopped
1 tsp dried oregano
1 tbsp freshly chopped fresh basil
400-g can organic tomatoes
1 tbsp fresh chopped parsley
410-g can no-salt mixed beans, drained and rinsed
FOR THE SALSA:
1 tbsp chopped yellow pepper
1 tbsp chopped green pepper
1 tbsp chopped red onion

1. Place the onions in a medium-sized saucepan with the olive oil and 1 tablespoon of water and cook for 2–3 minutes. Add the celery and leek and cook for a further 3–4 minutes.
2. Add the garlic and oregano, cook for 2 minutes, then add the basil and tomatoes and cook for a further 5 minutes.
3. Add 250 ml boiling water and the chopped parsley and cook for 5 more minutes, then add the beans.
4. To make the salsa, mix the peppers and red onion together in a small bowl.
5. Divide the soup between warmed bowls and serve garnished with the pepper salsa.

Sleepy lettuce soup

When I tell people to try lettuce soup, they look at me as if I've gone mad. It can taste delicious, I promise you, and has great health benefits. Lettuce has diuretic qualities and is therefore great for weight loss. It also helps dry up damp in the body – in other words, if you suffer from oedema, swollen ankles or yeasty problems such as thrush, lettuce is for you. Best of all, it contains a compound which is relaxing to the nervous system. So instead of counting sheep, try my Sleepy Lettuce Soup.

SERVES 4
1 tbsp olive oil
1 large onion, peeled and chopped
1 garlic clove, peeled and crushed
450 g potatoes, peeled and cut into 2-cm cubes
2 tsp wheat-free vegetable bouillon powder
8 tbsp millet
1 large romaine lettuce, washed and roughly shredded
4 tbsp chopped fresh chervil or parsley

1. Heat the oil with a little water in a large saucepan. Add the onion and garlic and cook for 3–4 minutes, stirring occasionally.

2. Add the potatoes and cook for 2 further minutes.

3. Add 1 litre water, together with the bouillon powder and millet. Bring to the boil, then lower the heat and simmer for 15 minutes or until the vegetables are tender when pierced with a knife.

4. Add the lettuce and cook for 2–3 minutes or until just wilted.

5. Allow to cool before blending in a food processor or with a hand-held blender until smooth along with 2 tablespoons of the fresh chervil or parsley.

6. Return to the pan to reheat, adding a little water if necessary.

7. Divide between warmed soup bowls and serve garnished with the remaining fresh chervil or parsley.

Courgette and asparagus soup

This soup is perfect for using up any left-over asparagus trimmings. Asparagus contains inulin, which can promote the growth and activity of intestine-friendly bacteria.

SERVES 4
1 onion, peeled and finely chopped
500 g courgettes, trimmed and cut into large pieces
1 bunch asparagus trimmings
1 ltr Roasted Vegetable Stock (see p.223)
1 handful fresh rosemary leaves
pumpkin oil or hemp oil

1. Place the onion with 1 tablespoon of water in a large pan and cook for 2–3 minutes. Add the courgettes, asparagus and the vegetable stock. Bring to the boil, then lower the heat and simmer for 10 minutes.
2. Allow to cool, then blend in a food processor or with a hand-held blender along with the fresh rosemary until smooth.
3. Divide between warmed soup bowls, drizzle over a little pumpkin or hemp oil and serve.

Fennel and hazelnut soup

Fennel contains a powerful combination of phytonutrients including anethole, which may enhance immune response. It is also an excellent source of vitamin C. Hazelnuts are rich in healthy fats.

SERVES 4
1 small onion, peeled and finely sliced
3 fennel bulbs, trimmed, finely sliced and cored
1 ltr Roasted Vegetable Stock (see p.223)
1 handful parsley stalks
100 g chopped hazelnuts (raw and unsalted)
soya milk

1. Place the onion with 1 tablespoon of water in a large pan and cook for 2–3 minutes. Add the fennel and vegetable stock. Bring to the boil, add the parsley stalks, then lower the heat and simmer for 20 minutes.

2. Allow to cool slightly then blend in a food processor or with a hand-held blender until completely smooth. Add the nuts and process for a further 30 seconds.

3. Return to the pan, adding a little soya milk to achieve a creamy consistency. Divide between warmed soup bowls and serve.

Warming split pea soup

This is my kids' favourite soup – they just can't get enough of it. Its ingredients help to strengthen digestion and the spleen, your energy battery. Great for cold winter days.

SERVES 4

225 g yellow split peas, presoaked for 12 hours or overnight in cold water
1 wheat-free vegetable stock cube
1 tsp wheat-free vegetable bouillon powder
1 onion, peeled and sliced
1 sweet potato, peeled and chopped
3 carrots, trimmed, peeled and thickly sliced
4 sprigs fresh mint
4 handfuls fresh baby spinach leaves

1. Place the presoaked peas in a sieve and rinse well in cold water. Transfer to a large saucepan and cover with 1.5 litres cold water, the stock cube and the bouillon powder. Bring to the boil, then lower the heat and simmer for 25 minutes. Remove any scum that rises to the surface with a spoon.

2. Add all the other vegetables and simmer for a further 15–20 minutes or until the vegetables are tender when pierced with a knife.

3. Remove from the heat and allow to cool, then blend the soup in a food processor or with a hand-held blender until smooth.

4. Return to the pan and reheat, stirring gently. Divide between warmed soup bowls, garnish with the fresh mint. Add the raw spinach leaves before serving.

Soups

Velvety cauliflower soup

SERVES 6

2 tbsp olive oil
2 garlic cloves, peeled and crushed
2 onions, peeled and chopped
3 leeks, washed, trimmed and sliced
half a celeriac, scrubbed, trimmed and chopped
1 cauliflower, trimmed and cut into small florets
1 tsp ground cumin (optional)
3 tbsp chopped fresh parsley

1. Heat the oil in a large saucepan or flameproof casserole
with 1 tablespoon of water over a low heat.
2. Add the garlic, onions, leeks and celeriac and cook very
gently for 20 minutes until softened, stirring occasionally.
3. Add the cauliflower florets, 1 litre cold water and the
cumin. Bring to the boil, then reduce the heat and simmer
for 10–15 minutes, stirring occasionally, until the cauliflower
is tender when pierced with a knife.
4. Leave to cool for 5 minutes then blend in a food processor
or with a hand-held blender until smooth. Return to the pan
and reheat gently. If necessary add more water (or Vegetable
Stock, see p.222).
5. Serve in warmed bowls and garnish with chopped
fresh parsley.

Tomato and herb soup with pearl barley

Tomatoes are rich in the antioxidant lycopene. Low levels of lycopene are associated with a higher risk of prostate cancer.

SERVES 4
100 g pearl barley
1 kg ripe tomatoes, chopped
1 onion, peeled and finely chopped
1 garlic clove, peeled and chopped
1 pinch grated fresh mace
1 handful fresh basil leaves and stalks
1 tsp chopped fresh oregano

1. Soak the pearl barley in cold water for 10 minutes. Drain and rinse well.

2. Place the tomatoes, onion, garlic and mace in a large pan and cook over a low heat for 20 minutes. Break up the tomatoes with a spoon as they cook.

3. Add 500 ml boiling water and basil stalks. Simmer for 10 minutes then remove from the heat and allow to cool.

4. Pass the mixture through a mouli or roughly blend in a food processor or with a hand held blender. Return to the pan and add the barley. Bring back to the boil, then lower the heat and simmer for 20 minutes. Add more water if required.

5. Divide between warm bowls and serve garnished with basil leaves and oregano.

SEVEN
SALADS &
LUNCH-BOXES

I highly recommend at least one salad a day for extra vitality. They are perfect for lunch and add that extra, raw zip to a cooked meal.

I remember filming with a family for the TV programme *You Are What You Eat* and being faced with the challenge that they all hated salad, particularly the eight-year-old son. Luckily, when I presented him with a crunchy alternative to limp lettuce leaves – beansprouts, yellow peppers, broccoli florets, cabbage shreds, beetroot shreds, radishes and chicory with a fennel and tomato dressing – he could not get enough. 'I've never had anything taste so good as this,' he said!

You can throw a tasty salad together in just a few minutes. As you'll see, there's much more to salads than lettuce, cucumber and tomato . . .

Avocado and barley salad with pumpkin seeds

A fantastic way to get a good supply of those fat-burning essential fatty acids and the ever-important sexy mineral zinc.

SERVES 4
2 ripe avocados
150 g cooked pot barley
100 g mangetout or sugar snap peas, trimmed
2 spring onions, trimmed and finely chopped
1 small bunch radishes, trimmed and sliced
1 tbsp chopped fresh parsley
1 tbsp pumpkin seeds
150 g mixed salad leaves
DRESSING:
2 tsp pumpkin oil
1 tsp freshly squeezed lemon juice

1. Peel, stone and slice the avocados and mix with the pot barley, mangetout or sugar snap peas, spring onions, radishes, parsley and pumpkin seeds.

2. Divide the salad leaves between salad plates and pile the avocado mixture on top.

3. Add 1 tablespoon of water to the salad dressing ingredients, mix together well and spoon a little dressing over each salad. Serve immediately.

Crunchy walnut coleslaw

This is a treat for your body. Cabbage contains compounds that help your liver to process toxins more effectively and walnuts have been found to help lower levels of bad cholesterol. Kohlrabi looks like a little turnip. It can be eaten raw in salads as here, used in soups or baked. So eat my crunchy coleslaw at least once a week.

SERVES 4

quarter of a white cabbage, cored and finely shredded
quarter of a kohlrabi, peeled and grated (optional)
4 carrots, trimmed, peeled and grated
2 celery stalks, trimmed and finely sliced
1 red pepper, deseeded and finely sliced
50 g fresh garden peas
3 spring onions, trimmed and finely sliced
100 g walnut halves
1 tbsp chopped fresh parsley
DRESSING:
3 tbsp olive oil
1 tbsp cider vinegar
1 tsp Dijon mustard
1 garlic clove, peeled and crushed

1. Combine all the vegetables for the coleslaw in a large bowl.
2. Using a food processor or hand-held blender, blend the dressing ingredients together with 3 tablespoons of water until creamy.
3. Pour the dressing over the salad and toss to combine.
4. Divide the salad between salad plates and serve garnished with the walnuts and parsley.

Salads and lunch-boxes

Haricot bean salad

This salad is full of fibre and a rich source of vitamin B, essential for weight management and the nervous system. Cider vinegar is excellent for digestion.

SERVES 4

250g fresh haricot beans, presoaked for 12 hours or overnight in cold water
1 onion, peeled and finely chopped
1 tsp miso paste
1 wheat-free vegetable stock cube
1 celery stalk, trimmed and finely sliced
3 tbsp chopped pickled gherkins and silverskin onions
half a red pepper, deseeded and finely sliced
half a yellow pepper, deseeded and finely sliced
100 g sauerkraut
125 g mixed baby leaves
2 tbsp sunflower seeds
4 tbsp chopped fresh parsley
DRESSING:
1 tbsp olive oil
1 tsp cider vinegar

1. Bring a litre of water to the boil in a large pan and add the beans, onion, miso and stock cube. Bring back to the boil, then lower the heat and simmer for 20–30 minutes, until the beans are soft but not breaking up. Drain.

2. Add 1 tablespoon of water to the dressing ingredients, mix well and toss in to the beans.

3. Mix the celery, pickled gherkins and silverskin onions, peppers and sauerkraut together and arrange with the salad leaves on a large platter.

4. Scatter the beans over the salad and serve garnished with sunflower seeds and plenty of parsley.

Salads and lunch-boxes

Spring salad

I use the Chinese root daikon in this salad. I have found it to be helpful for congestion. Asparagus is often used to help with PMS-related water retention.

SERVES 4

100 g mangetout
1 bunch asparagus, trimmed and cut into bite-sized pieces
1 carrot, trimmed, peeled and cut into thin julienne (matchstick) strips
quarter of a daikon or mooli, peeled and cut into large julienne (matchstick) strips
1 bunch radishes, trimmed and cut into quarters
75 g pumpkin seeds
10 g shelled hemp seeds
DRESSING:
1 tsp umeboshi paste
2 tbsp rice malt
2 tsp olive oil

1. Bring a large pot of water to the boil and blanch the vegetables one at a time, starting with the mangetout and asparagus, which need to be cooked for 2–3 minutes, then the carrot for 3–4 minutes and finally the daikon or mooli for 4–5 minutes. Remove each vegetable as it is cooked with a slotted spoon and refresh under cold water. Drain well.
2. Add 1 tablespoon of water to the dressing ingredients and mix well.
3. In a large salad bowl mix the cooked vegetables with the radishes. Spoon over the dressing and serve garnished with the pumpkin and hemp seeds.

Tabbouleh

I use buckwheat groats in my tabbouleh as they are gluten-free, so easy on the digestive tract. I also use lots of parsley – it's one of the most important herbs for providing vitamins to your body and is also an excellent digestive restorative.

SERVES 4

175 g buckwheat groats
6 tbsp chopped fresh mint
12 tbsp chopped fresh parsley
1 large beef tomato, halved, deseeded and finely chopped
1 cucumber, peeled, deseeded and diced
2 onions, peeled and finely chopped
1 tbsp olive oil
juice of 1 lemon
1 pinch of dried mixed herbs
lettuce leaves
4 lemon wedges

1. Rinse and drain the buckwheat groats. Bring a medium-sized pan of water to the boil, add the buckwheat groats and cook for 10 minutes or until tender. Drain and allow to cool.
2. Mix the mint, parsley, tomato, cucumber, onion, olive oil, lemon juice and dried mixed herbs together in a large bowl. Mix through the buckwheat groats and chill until required.
3. Pile high on a serving platter and serve garnished with lettuce and lemon wedges.

Sea vegetable and sprouts salad

The idea of eating seaweed in a salad may seem wacky at first glance. The reality is that sea vegetables can offer a wonderful complement to many meals, both in taste and nutrition. Wakame is sweet in flavour and a good source of calcium.

SERVES 4

2 strips wakame sea vegetable
half a cucumber, peeled and cut into julienne
(matchstick) strips
1 punnet cherry tomatoes, halved
1 baby gem lettuce, leaves separated
100 g canned sweetcorn, drained and rinsed
250 g mung bean sprouts
DRESSING:
1 tsp soy or tamari sauce
1 tbsp olive oil
1 tbsp orange rind
1 tsp grated fresh ginger root
2 tbsp freshly pressed apple juice

1. Rinse the wakame under cold water for 1 minute, then soak in a bowl of cold water for 2–3 minutes.
2. Place the dressing ingredients in a small bowl, add 3 tablespoons of water and whisk well to combine.
3. Drain the wakame and chop into bite-sized pieces. Place in a small bowl with half the dressing and leave to marinate.
4. Arrange the remaining ingredients in a large salad bowl, add the wakame and the rest of the dressing, toss the salad and serve immediately.

Warm vegetable quinoa salad

Quinoa is a supergrain and contains all the essential amino acids as well as being a rich source of calcium.

SERVES 4

1 red pepper, deseeded and halved
1 yellow pepper, deseeded and halved
1 courgette, trimmed and finely sliced
1 small red onion, peeled and finely sliced
60 g quinoa grains
2 tbsp pine nuts
4 sprigs fresh thyme
2 sprigs fresh rosemary
100 g fresh rocket
3 tbsp chopped fresh basil
4 lemon wedges

1. Preheat the oven to 200C/gas mark 6.

2. Place the peppers cut side up on an ovenproof baking dish and scatter the courgette and red onion over the top. Place in the oven and roast for 15 minutes.

3. Meanwhile, rinse and drain the quinoa and add to a medium-sized pan of boiling water, along with the thyme and rosemary. Cook for 8–10 minutes. Drain and put aside.

4. Scatter 1 tablespoon of the pine nuts over the peppers and cook for a further 5–10 minutes.

5. Remove the baking dish from the oven and spoon the quinoa into the pepper halves.

6. Scatter with rocket, fresh basil and the remaining pine nuts and arrange the lemon wedges (for squeezing) on the top. Serve immediately.

Warm chicken salad

SERVES 4
2 skinless organic chicken breasts
75 g green beans, trimmed
75 g asparagus spears
6 cherry tomatoes, halved
2 tbsp pine nuts
4 tbsp chopped fresh basil
1 handful baby salad leaves
DRESSING:
2 tbsp extra virgin olive oil
1 tsp cider vinegar
1 tsp Dijon mustard

1. Place the chicken in a small pan of cold water, bring
to the boil, then lower the heat and simmer for 8–10 minutes.
Remove from the pan and allow to cool slightly. Alternatively
steam in a steamer.
2. Steam the green beans and asparagus spears until tender
but still crisp; refresh in cold water.
3. Mix the beans and asparagus with all the other salad
ingredients in a bowl except for the baby salad leaves.
4. Place the dressing ingredients in a screw-top jar with
1 tablespoon of water and shake well.
5. Slice the chicken while still warm and add to the salad.
Pour over the dressing and toss to coat.
6. Serve in a large salad bowl, garnished with the baby
salad leaves.

Salads and lunch-boxes

Salad niçoise

SERVES 4
100-g piece fresh tuna
1 bunch asparagus tips
4 baby gem lettuces
200 g baby spinach leaves
2 tbsp black olives
150 g cherry tomatoes, halved
2 hard-boiled eggs, shelled and cut in quarters (optional)
DRESSING:
1 tsp Dijon mustard
1 tbsp olive oil
2 tsp cider vinegar

1. Heat a griddle or non-stick pan on high heat until very
hot. Add the tuna and sear for 2–3 minutes. With a spatula
turn the tuna over and cook for a further 2–3 minutes.
2. Bring a small pan of water to the boil, add the asparagus
and cook for 2 minutes. Remove from the heat, drain and
refresh in plenty of cold water.
3. Arrange the lettuce leaves, spinach, olives, tomatoes
and asparagus tips on a platter. Break up the tuna and
place on the leaves. Add the egg if using.
4. For the dressing mix the mustard with 1 teaspoon of
water, then whisk in the oil and vinegar. Drizzle over the
salad and serve.

Grated carrot and courgette coleslaw

SERVES 4
3 carrots, trimmed, peeled and grated
2 courgettes, trimmed and cut into
fine julienne (matchstick) strips or grated
2 spring onions, trimmed and finely diced
1 tsp cider vinegar
1 tbsp egg-free mayonnaise
2 tbsp pumpkin seeds

1. Mix the carrots, courgettes and spring onions in
a medium-sized mixing bowl.
2. Mix the cider vinegar with the mayonnaise and then
mix in with the coleslaw ingredients. Cover and chill
until required.
3. Serve garnished with the pumpkin seeds.

Cucumber, dulse and avocado salad

Dulse is a seaweed vegetable that has a nutty flavour, a great addition to salads.

SERVES 4
30 g dulse sea vegetable
2 avocados
1 cucumber, peeled and finely sliced
1 carrot, trimmed, peeled and grated
125 g natural sauerkraut
1 handful chopped fresh chives
1 small bunch watercress, trimmed and cut into
bite-sized pieces
2 tbsp freshly pressed apple juice
zest of 1 lemon
juice of half a lemon

1. Rinse the dulse in cold water and soak for 2–3 minutes. Drain and squeeze out the excess water. Chop into bite-sized pieces.

2. Peel and stone the avocados, and cut into small pieces.

3. Mix the dulse and avocado with all the other ingredients in a large salad bowl and serve.

Warm red lentil salad

Red lentils help strengthen the adrenal glands and kidneys. They are also a rich source of fibre, which makes them great additions to any weight-loss programme.

SERVES 4
100 g red lentils
2 shallots, peeled and chopped
1 garlic clove, peeled and crushed
1 tsp chopped fresh root ginger
2 tsp wheat-free vegetable bouillon powder
100 g fresh mixed salad leaves, including rocket and/or baby spinach leaves
2 tbsp chopped fresh coriander or mint
4 lime wedges

1. Rinse and drain the lentils and place in a medium-sized saucepan. Add the shallots, garlic, root ginger and bouillon powder and cover in cold water. Bring to the boil, then lower the heat and simmer for 10–15 minutes, or until tender. Stir occasionally.

2. Remove from the heat and drain away the excess water.

3. Divide the salad leaves between serving plates and pile the red lentils on top.

4. Garnish with the coriander or mint and lime wedges (for squeezing) and serve.

Green salad

SERVES 4
2 tbsp pine nuts
1 ripe avocado, stoned, peeled and sliced
half a cucumber, finely sliced
1 celery stalk, trimmed and finely sliced
100 g watercress
100 g rocket
1 baby gem lettuce, leaves whole
DRESSING:
1 tsp Dijon mustard
1 tbsp cider vinegar
2 tbsp olive oil

1. Place the pine nuts in a small pan over a low heat and toast, stirring frequently until golden in colour. Set aside.

2. Mix the dressing ingredients together in a large salad bowl.

3. Add the avocado to the dressing and toss, then pile the other salad ingredients, except the pine nuts, on top.

4. Just before serving toss the salad and sprinkle with the pine nuts.

Seaweed salad

SERVES 4
50 g mixed seaweed
200 g red or yellow cherry tomatoes, halved
2 spring onions, trimmed and finely sliced
100 g rocket
1 red endive
1 tbsp pumpkin seeds
DRESSING:
1 tbsp cider vinegar
2 tsp pumpkin oil

1. Soak the seaweed for 10 minutes in cold water then drain well.

2. Mix the seaweed with the tomatoes and spring onions. Place the rocket in a salad bowl and top with the seaweed mixture. Arrange the endive leaves around the edge of the salad.

3. Mix the dressing ingredients together and pour over the salad. Serve garnished with the pumpkin seeds.

Wild rice salad with beetroot

SERVES 4
100 g brown rice
100 g wild rice
4 shallots, peeled and halved
2 tsp olive oil
4 cooked beetroot, finely diced
juice of 1 lemon
2 tbsp chopped fresh mint
2 tbsp chopped fresh parsley
2 tbsp chopped fresh chives

1. Preheat the oven to 200C/gas mark 6.
2. Place the brown and wild rice in a medium-sized pan of water. Bring to the boil, then lower the heat and simmer for 20 minutes.
3. Place the shallots in a small pan, cover with water and bring to the boil. Cook for 2 minutes, remove from the heat and allow to cool then drain.
4. Place the shallots on a baking tray, drizzle with oil and roast for 5 minutes.
5. Drain the rice and allow to cool. Mix with the beetroot, lemon juice and mint.
6. Stir in the shallots, parsley and chives and serve.

Broccoli salad with apple vinaigrette

SERVES 4

1 head broccoli, cut into florets
2 courgettes, trimmed and cut into fine julienne
(matchstick) strips
2 celery stalks, trimmed and cut on the diagonal
1 small bunch radishes, trimmed and quartered

APPLE VINAIGRETTE:

1 tbsp Dijon mustard
2 tbsp white miso paste or 1 tbsp wheat-free tamari
1 tsp toasted sesame oil
3 tbsp freshly pressed apple juice

1. Bring a medium-sized saucepan of water to the boil.
Add the broccoli and blanch for 2–3 minutes. Strain and
run under the cold water tap until completely cold.

2. Place the broccoli in a salad bowl with the courgettes,
celery and radishes.

3. Place the vinaigrette ingredients in a screw-top jar
and shake well to blend.

4. Pour the vinaigrette over the salad and serve.

Goat's cheese salad with roasted tomatoes, peppers and rocket

Goat's cheese is a good source of calcium and also potassium, a mineral which helps to maintain normal blood pressure. Perhaps the greatest benefit is for people who cannot tolerate dairy products, most of whom are usually able to eat goat's cheese without any problems. Enjoy this recipe as a special treat.

SERVES 4
4 red peppers, deseeded and halved
12 cherry tomatoes
2 tsp olive oil
125 g goat's cheese, crumbled
2 tbsp pine nuts
200 g rocket
2 tbsp chopped fresh basil

1. Preheat the oven to 200C/gas mark 6.
2. Place the peppers (cutside up) and tomatoes on a baking tray, drizzle with olive oil and roast for 10 minutes. Sprinkle the goat's cheese inside the peppers and cook for a further 5 minutes.
3. Scatter over the pine nuts and return to the oven for 5 more minutes.
4. Arrange the rocket on 4 plates, top with the peppers and tomatoes. Serve garnished with the fresh basil.

LUNCH-BOXES

After years of working with clients, I have found that there are two major issues that surround lunch: most people are at a loss as to what they should eat when it comes to lunch time and many people simply eat lunch far too late in the day.

First, I want you to eat a lot of food at lunch time. Second, I want you to eat this ample lunch at roughly the same time each day for regulation of your internal body clock. Always eat your lunch sometime between noon and 1:30pm at the latest, so that you don't disrupt your blood sugar-glucose balance. One of the biggest problems that I have found in practice is that clients often complain of massive energy slumps mid or late afternoon. This is directly related to lunch – either they are not eating enough, they are eating sweets and junk food, or just waiting too long to eat and conjuring up excuses as to why there's no time.

Make the time to prepare for lunch and proper time to actually eat your lunch. Even if you have to get foods ready the night before, then so be it. It really will be worth it. Here we go with my easy lunch box ideas.

01

Bunch of red grapes (always eat your fruit first –
it might seem a bit strange initially, but your digestion
will thank you)
Flask of soup (see pp.96–113)
Salad Niçoise (p.124) or make a simple salad of tuna,
hard-boiled egg (optional), baby spinach leaves and
green beans
Veggie crudités and Home-Made Houmous (p.205)
Pumpkin seeds

02

Melon slices
Butter Bean Spread (p.200) with variety of crunchy
raw veggies
Corn on the cob (cook the night before and store in
the fridge in an airtight container)
Soaked almonds

03

Banana or small punnet of berries
Flask of soup
Wild Rice Salad (p.130)
Veggie crudités and Sesame Squash Spread (p.198)
Sunflower seeds

04

2 nectarines
Flask of soup
Toasted Nori Strips (p.209)
Sliced chicken breast with cherry tomatoes, rocket
and Crunchy Walnut Coleslaw (p.117)
Hemp seeds and pumpkin seeds

05

Peach
Flask of soup
Cous cous and Grated Carrot and Courgette Coleslaw (p. 125)
Rice cakes with Black Olive Tapenade (p.203)

EIGHT
MAIN MEALS

These are some of my favourite recipes and have been a real hit with my clients. They are bursting with nutrients and will keep you looking and feeling fantastic. What's more, they're simple to prepare and cook – minimum effort for great results!

Chickpea burgers

These are a hit in any household. As well as making a meal in themselves, any mini-burgers left over can be used in a lunch-box or as a snack. Kids love them – and they're healthy too. Chickpeas have a naturally sweet flavour, are a good source of iron, good fats and nutritionally help out the tummy and heart. I have combined them with sunflower seeds – power-packed with EFAs, minerals and B vitamins for an energy pick-me-up.

MAKES 20
410-g can chickpeas, drained and rinsed
410-g can red kidney beans, drained and rinsed
1 carrot, trimmed, peeled and finely grated
1 small onion, peeled and finely grated
50 g sunflower seeds
2 tbsp tahini, drained of any excess oil before measuring
1 garlic clove, peeled and chopped
1 handful chopped fresh coriander
1 tbsp wheat-free vegetable bouillon powder

1. Preheat the oven to 220C/gas mark 7. Line a large baking tray with greaseproof paper.
2. Place all the ingredients in a food processor or with a hand-held blender and blend for 5–10 seconds, until the mixture is fairly coarse. Push the mixture down with a spatula and blend for a further 10 seconds.
3. Remove the blades from the processor, wet your hands under the cold water tap and shape the mixture into 20 small balls.
4. Place the balls on the prepared baking tray and flatten slightly with the back of the spoon.
5. Bake for 15–18 minutes until lightly coloured. Remove from the oven and allow to rest. Serve with Sweet Potato Wedges (see p.206) and a crunchy raw salad of mangetout, radishes, grated carrot, sliced celery and fennel dressed with a squeeze of lemon juice.

Chicken burgers

Try to buy free-range, organic chicken.

MAKES 6
500 g skinless organic chicken breasts, chilled
3 spring onions, trimmed and sliced
1 garlic clove, peeled and chopped
2 tbsp chopped fresh parsley
1 tsp organic wheat-free vegetable bouillon powder
2 baby gem lettuces
200 g cherry tomatoes, halved
1 carrot, trimmed, peeled and grated
half a cucumber, trimmed and sliced
half a red pepper, trimmed, deseeded and sliced
half a yellow pepper, trimmed, deseeded and sliced

1. Preheat the oven to 200C/gas mark 6. Line a baking
tray with aluminium foil.

2. Cut the chicken breasts into chunks, then place in a
food processor and blend for 1 minute. Add the spring onions,
garlic and parsley and blend for a further 30 seconds.

3. Dissolve the bouillon powder in 1 tablespoon of hot water
and add to the chicken mixture.Blend for 30 seconds to allow
the mixture to form a soft ball.

4. Remove from the food processor and place in a clean bowl.
Cover and chill for 30 minutes.

5. Wet your hands under the cold water tap and shape the
mixture into 6 even-sized balls. Place on the prepared baking
tray and lightly depress with the back of a spoon to form
burger shapes.

6. Place in the preheated oven and cook for 5–7 minutes.
Turn the burgers over and cook for a further 5–10 minutes.

7. Remove from the oven and allow to rest for 5 minutes.
Place each burger on two gem lettuce leaves and top with
tomatoes, grated carrot, cucumber and pepper slices.
Serve with my Tangy Barbecue Relish (see p.224).

Main meals

139

Steamed apple chicken

This is a good transitional dish for people who are changing from really sweet, overly processed diets to a more wholesome diet. The extra sweetness provided by the apple juice facilitates the changeover. It's best served with beansprouts for a boost of energy-giving food enzymes that also help improve digestion.

SERVES 4

4 skinless organic chicken breasts
2 tsp avocado or olive oil
3-cm piece fresh root ginger, peeled and finely chopped
2 garlic cloves, peeled and chopped
2 small onions, peeled and finely diced
2 carrots, trimmed, peeled and finely diced
1 small red pepper, deseeded and finely diced
1 head broccoli, cut into small florets
20 baby corn, trimmed
250 ml freshly pressed apple juice
100 g raw beansprouts

1. Preheat the oven to 200C/gas mark 6.
2. Take a large piece of aluminium foil and place the chicken breasts in the centre. Drizzle over the oil and add the ginger, garlic and vegetables. Draw up the sides of the foil and pour in the apple juice.
3. Scrunch up the foil to seal everything in and place in the oven for 25 minutes.
4. Remove from the oven and allow to rest for 5 minutes.
5. Divide the contents of the foil parcel between four serving plates and serve immediately with the raw bean sprouts and a large salad.

Baked butterflied chicken with shiitake mushrooms

Shiitake mushrooms are a superb immune system tonic. Even people who suffer from yeasty conditions, and normally have to avoid mushrooms, can eat shiitakes as they contain substances which can lower nasty yeasties and bacteria.

SERVES 4
1 tbsp olive oil
4 skinless organic chicken breasts
125 g shiitake mushrooms, trimmed
1 garlic clove, peeled and chopped
4 shallots, peeled and finely chopped
2 tbsp chopped fresh parsley
1 tbsp wheat-free vegetable bouillon powder dissolved in 100 ml hot water
12 cherry tomatoes
4 small sprigs fresh thyme
4 small sprigs fresh rosemary
1 lemon, cut into 4 wedges

1. Preheat the oven to 200C/gas mark 6.
2. Take four large pieces of aluminium foil and oil each centre with a pastry brush.
3. With a sharp knife carefully slice through the centre of each chicken breast horizontally to form a pocket. Do not cut all the way through.
4. Fill the pockets with the mushrooms, garlic, shallots and parsley. Place each one on an oiled foil, draw up the sides and add 25ml bouillon water, 3 cherry tomatoes and 1 sprig of thyme and rosemary to each pocket. Squeeze a little lemon over each.
5. Scrunch up the foil to seal everything in and place on a baking tray in the oven for 25 minutes.
6. Remove from the oven and allow to rest for 5 minutes.
7. Transfer the foil parcels to four serving plates, open the parcels slightly and serve immediately with a large salad.

Tempeh with kale, radishes and sauerkraut

Kale is an exceptional source of chlorophyll, iron, calcium and other minerals, a superveg. I often use radishes in soups, too, to help prevent colds and clear the sinuses. And my favourite, sauerkraut, is very good for the liver.

SERVES 4

70 g tempeh
1 strip kombu sea vegetable
2 tsp tamari sauce
2.5cm-piece fresh root ginger, peeled and finely sliced
250-g pack curly kale
1 tsp olive oil
1 small bunch radishes, trimmed and cut in half
3–4 tbsp natural sauerkraut
1 tbsp pumpkin seeds

1. Cut the tempeh into 4 pieces and place in a medium-sized pan with the kombu, tamari sauce and fresh ginger. Pour in enough water to half-cover the tempeh. Bring to the boil, then lower the heat and simmer for 10 minutes. Remove from the heat and allow to cool.

2. Bring a medium-sized pan of water to the boil, add the kale and boil for 3–4 minutes. Drain and rinse in cold water.

3. Strain and slice the tempeh, discarding the kombu and ginger.

4. Heat the oil in a small frying pan with 1 tablespoon of water, add the tempeh and pan-fry for a few seconds.

5. Arrange the kale, radishes and sauerkraut on a serving platter, top with the tempeh and serve garnished with the pumpkin seeds.

Dr Gillian's shepherdess pie

Root veggies strengthen and improve digestion. Always serve with plenty of raw salad leaves.

SERVES 4

4 sweet potatoes, peeled and roughly chopped
2 tsp olive oil
1 garlic clove, peeled and crushed
2 celery stalks, trimmed and finely sliced
1 onion, peeled and finely sliced
350 g butternut squash, peeled, deseeded and chopped
450 ml Roasted Vegetable Stock (see p.223)
410-g can kidney beans, drained and rinsed
410-g can black-eye peas, drained and rinsed
2 red peppers, deseeded and sliced
2 courgettes, trimmed and sliced
4 tomatoes, sliced in half
1 dessertspoonful arrowroot powder
2 tbsp chopped fresh parsley

1. Preheat the oven to 200C/gas mark 6.

2. Steam or boil the sweet potatoes for 10–15 minutes until completely tender.

3. Place 2 tablespoons of water in a medium-sized saucepan with the oil, garlic, celery and onion and cook for 3 minutes. Add the squash and cook for a further 2 minutes, stirring frequently. Add the stock and bring to the boil. Cover, lower the heat and simmer for 10 minutes.

4. Add the beans, peas, peppers, courgettes and tomatoes and simmer for a further 5 minutes.

5. Mix the arrowroot with a little water and add along with the parsley.

6. Drain the sweet potato and mash.

7. Transfer the filling to a pie dish and top with the sweet potato mash.

8. Bake for 12–15 minutes until the sweet potato begins to brown. Serve immediately with a green salad.

Main meals

Lettuce and cashew nut wraps with tahini dressing

Lettuce is great on a weight-loss programme because it's a diuretic. It's also a calming food and can even help dry up dampness in the body caused by yeast and bacteria brought on by poor digestion. Have a look at your tongue in the mirror. If there's a white or yellow coating, a line down the middle or cuts or serrations at the very back, then it's lettuce to the rescue. These wraps are also perfect for packed lunches (see p.134). Try some of your own fillings – chopped cooked chicken or flaked tuna make good alternatives to the cashew nuts.

MAKES 6
6 large lettuce leaves (Cos, iceberg or oak leaf)
1 carrot, trimmed, peeled and cut into fine julienne (matchstick) strips
1 red pepper, deseeded and finely sliced
2 spring onions, trimmed and finely sliced
2 tbsp chopped red onion
75 g cashew nuts, roughly chopped
75 g beansprouts
2 tbsp tamari sauce
DRESSING:
3 tbsp tahini
1 tbsp cider vinegar

1. Prepare the dressing by mixing the tahini and cider vinegar together with 3 tablespoons of cold water in a small mixing bowl.

2. Arrange the salad leaves on a large platter.

3. In a bowl, mix together all the other ingredients and divide between the lettuce leaves. Spoon a little of the dressing over the filling. Roll the leaves around the filling and secure with a toothpick.

4. Serve the wraps with the remaining dressing to the side.

Haricot bean loaf

Haricot beans are an excellent source of protein and support
kidney-adrenal function, metabolism and regulation of
blood sugar levels.

SERVES 4
2 tsp olive oil
1 leek, washed, trimmed and sliced
2.5-cm piece fresh root ginger, peeled and grated
half teaspoon ground cumin
half teaspoon ground coriander
1 onion, peeled and quartered
3 carrots, trimmed, peeled and grated
1 garlic clove, peeled and chopped
3 tbsp chopped fresh parsley
50 g sunflower seeds
24 g oat bran
1 tbsp wheat-free vegetable bouillon powder
410-g can haricot beans, drained and rinsed
410-g can red kidney beans, drained and rinsed

1. Preheat the oven to 190C/gas mark 5. Lightly oil
a 900-g loaf tin and line the base with greaseproof paper.
2. Put the remaining oil and the leek in a small saucepan
and cook over a low heat for 5 minutes. Add the ginger,
cumin and coriander and cook for a further minute.
Remove from the heat and allow to cool.
3. Place the onion, carrots, garlic, parsley, sunflower seeds,
oat bran, bouillon powder and one of the cans of beans
(either will do) in a food processor and blend for 20 seconds
until semi-smooth. Transfer into a large bowl and stir in
the second can of beans and the leek mixture.
4. Spoon into the prepared tin and bake for 40–45 minutes
until golden brown in colour.
5. Turn out of the tin on to a serving plate. Serve either
hot or cold with a lightly dressed salad.

Main meals

145

Mediterranean black-eye pea casserole

A fantastic adrenal-strengthener and fibre-rich meal.

SERVES 4
1 tbsp olive oil
1 garlic clove, peeled and finely chopped
2 onions, peeled and finely sliced
410-g can black-eye peas, drained and rinsed
3 tomatoes, quartered
100 g shiitake mushrooms, trimmed and quartered
2 carrots, trimmed, peeled and diced
1 tbsp chopped fresh basil
1 tsp dried oregano
1 tsp dried marjoram
2 tsp tamari sauce
2 courgettes, trimmed and cut into fine julienne
(matchstick) strips
1 tsp capers (optional)
1 tbsp each chopped fresh basil, oregano and parsley

1. Heat the oil in a medium-sized casserole dish on the hob.
Add the garlic and onion and cook for a couple of minutes.
Add the peas, tomatoes, mushrooms, carrots, herbs and
tamari. Bring to the boil, then lower the heat and simmer
for 10–15 minutes. When cooked, the vegetables should
still have a little bite. Add a little water or stock if required
during the cooking process.
2. Remove from the heat and add the courgettes. Serve
from the casserole dish and garnish with the capers,
if using, and the fresh herbs. Accompany with Gourmet
Brown Rice (see p.185) and a side salad.

Baked salmon with spinach and leeks

More than two-thirds of the people who come to see me for the first time test deficient in omega-3 fats. This dish provides plenty through the avocado and salmon.

SERVES 4
2 leeks, washed, trimmed and sliced
500 g fresh baby spinach leaves
four 100-g organic salmon fillets
1 tbsp olive oil
2 garlic cloves, peeled and finely chopped
1 tbsp grated fresh root ginger
juice of half a lemon
1 handful fresh coriander leaves, to garnish

1. Preheat the oven to 200C/gas mark 6.
2. Gently boil or steam the leeks for 5 minutes to soften.
3. Place the spinach leaves in a medium-sized baking tin and top with the leeks. Place the salmon on the top.
4. Mix together the oil, garlic and ginger and liberally brush over the salmon using a pastry brush. Pour over the lemon juice.
5. Place in the oven and bake for 10 minutes. Remove and allow to rest for 5 minutes. Garnish with fresh coriander leaves and serve with Avocado Dressing (see p.159) drizzled over the top.

Mackerel with pine nuts and parsley

Many of us don't get nearly enough good fats in our diet, and they are plentiful in this recipe. Pine nuts are also helpful to the lungs, colon and intestines, while parsley is a herbal 'multivitamin' and excellent for good digestion. What more could you possibly ask for in a dish?

SERVES 4
4 whole mackerel, scaled and gutted
1 garlic clove, peeled and sliced
4 tbsp chopped fresh parsley
8 lemon slices
FILLING:
4 spring onions, trimmed and chopped
3 tbsp roughly chopped pine nuts
3 tbsp chopped fresh parsley
zest of 1 lemon
1 garlic clove, peeled and chopped
GARNISH:
1 handful mixed salad leaves
6 cherry tomatoes, halved
quarter of a cucumber sliced
half a yellow pepper, deseeded and finely sliced
4 lemon wedges

1. Preheat the grill as high as possible. Cover the grill pan in aluminium foil.
2. With a sharp knife make two incisions in the side of each mackerel. Fill the incisions with garlic and parsley and place on the tray.
3. Combine the filling ingredients together in a small bowl and use to stuff the cavity of the fish.

4. Arrange the lemon slices over the fish. Place under the hot grill and cook for 3–4 minutes. Turn the mackerel over and repeat on the second side.

5. Remove from under the grill and allow the fish to rest for 5 minutes. Divide the salad garnish ingredients and lemon wedges (for squeezing) between 4 plates, add the mackerel and serve.

Baked fish with carrot and leek purée

Leeks are in the same family as onions and garlic and so have the same health benefits, including anti-cancer properties, helping lower 'bad' cholesterol (LDL) while raising 'good' cholesterol (HDL) and stabilizing blood sugar levels.

SERVES 4
4 carrots, trimmed, peeled and sliced
1 leek, washed, trimmed and sliced
1 tbsp wheat-free vegetable bouillon powder
four 100-g white fish fillets such as haddock or whiting
4 tsp olive oil, plus extra to glaze
100 g fresh garden peas
2 tbsp chopped fresh mint
100 g fresh watercress
100 g fresh rocket

1. Preheat the oven to 200C/gas mark 6.

2. Place the carrots and leek in a medium- to large-sized saucepan. Add the bouillon powder and enough boiling water to cover. Bring back to the boil, then lower the heat and allow to simmer for approximately 10–15 minutes, or until tender when pierced with a knife. Allow to cool slightly, then blend in a food processor or with a hand-held blender until smooth.

3. Line a baking tray with aluminium foil and place the fish on it. Using a pastry brush glaze the fish with olive oil.

4. Transfer to the oven and bake for 8–10 minutes.

5. Bring a small pan of water to the boil and add the peas. Cook for 2–3 minutes then drain, reserving about 1 tablespoon of the juice. Add the 4 tsp oil and the mint and crush the peas with the back of a fork.

6. Take 4 warmed serving plates and divide the purée between them. Place the fish on the purée and then spoon the pea mixture on top. Garnish with loads of watercress and rocket and serve immediately.

Salmon with orange and soy sauce

SERVES 4

4 tbsp tamari sauce
zest and juice of 1 orange
2-cm piece fresh root ginger, peeled and finely chopped
1 garlic clove, peeled and crushed
4 spring onions, trimmed and sliced
four 150-g organic salmon fillets
1 orange, finely sliced
200 g mixed baby spinach, watercress and rocket leaves

1. Preheat the oven to 200C/gas mark 6.
2. Mix together the tamari, zest and juice of the orange, ginger, garlic and spring onions in a shallow glass ovenproof pie dish. Add the salmon, cover in cling film and marinate in the fridge for 30 minutes, turning occasionally.
3. Uncover the dish and arrange the orange slices on the top.
4. Bake for 10–15 minutes until the fish is firm to the touch. Remove from the oven and allow to stand for 5 minutes.
5. Arrange the salad leaves on the plates and top with the salmon. Pour over the cooking juices. Serve with lightly steamed vegetables.

Chestnut roast

This recipe is perfect for the weekend or a special occasion.

SERVES 4

1 tbsp olive oil, plus extra to grease the tin
1 large red onion, peeled and finely chopped
3 garlic cloves, peeled and crushed
1 large leek, washed, trimmed and sliced
2 carrots, trimmed, peeled and sliced
1 large parsnip, trimmed, peeled and chopped
200 g vacuum-packed chestnuts
100 g pine nuts
3 tbsp chopped fresh parsley
2 tbsp chopped fresh thyme
2 tsp finely chopped fresh rosemary
2 tsp wheat-free vegetable bouillon powder
100 g soft mild goat's cheese (optional)
fresh rosemary sprigs and bay leaves

1. Preheat the oven to 180C/gas mark 4.
2. Take a 24-cm ring-shaped cake tin and use to cut out a
circle of greaseproof paper. Cut a hole in the centre of the
paper 2 cm larger than the hole in the tin. Make 1-cm cuts,
3 cm apart, around the inside and outside of the paper circle.
Brush the tin with a little olive oil, line with the paper and
brush with a little more oil.
3. Heat 1 tablespoon olive oil in a large frying pan.
Gently cook the onion and garlic for 3–5 minutes, stirring
occasionally until softened but not coloured. Add the leek,
carrots and parsnip with 375 ml water. Bring to the boil,
then lower the heat and simmer for 6–8 minutes. The water
will have evaporated and the vegetables should be tender
when pierced with a knife. Allow to cool in the pan for
10 minutes.

4. Place the chestnuts in the food processor and blend for 10–15 seconds until roughly chopped. Transfer to a large bowl and add the vegetables, pine nuts, parsley, thyme, rosemary and bouillon powder. Mix well and spoon half the mixture into the prepared ring mould, pressing down well. Dot with half the cheese, if using, and then top with the remaining vegetable mixture. Dot with the rest of the cheese.

5. Bake for 40–45 minutes until lightly browned. Remove from the oven and allow to cool in the tin for 5 minutes. Carefully loosen with a palette knife and turn out on to a warmed serving plate. Garnish with the fresh rosemary sprigs and bay leaves.

Haricot bean and root vegetable stew

A good source of fibre and those important B vitamins that are necessary for weight management and strong nervous systems.

SERVES 4
1 tbsp olive oil
2 onions, peeled and diced
2 bay leaves
half a swede, trimmed, peeled and diced
3 carrots, trimmed, peeled and cut in large chunks
half a red pepper, deseeded and finely sliced
410-g can haricot beans, drained and rinsed
half teaspoon cumin seeds
1 tbsp white miso paste
2 tbsp chopped fresh parsley
50 g beansprouts
4 spring onions, trimmed and finely sliced

1. Heat a large casserole dish and add the oil, onion, bay leaves and a little water. Cook for 10 minutes until soft but not coloured. Add the swede, carrots and pepper and enough water to cover. Bring to the boil, then reduce the heat and simmer gently for 10 minutes.
2. Stir in the beans, cumin and white miso and simmer for a further 10 minutes.
3. Serve immediately, garnished with the parsley, beansprouts and spring onions.

Smoked tofu and bean burgers

Kidney beans are a good source of iron, magnesium and folate. This recipe makes six chunky burgers that are ideal for a light lunch for six, or eight smaller burgers that would make a more generous meal for four people. Serve your burgers with one of my delicious raw side salads or some raw veggies. Never forget to do that. With every dish that is cooked, you need to complement it with some raw vegetables, leaves or herbs to aid digestion and food's enzymes into the body.

MAKES 6–8
1 onion, peeled and quartered
1 garlic clove, peeled and chopped
1 carrot, trimmed, peeled and grated
410-g can red kidney beans, drained and rinsed
220 g smoked tofu, cut in 2-cm cubes
75 g sunflower seeds
1 small bunch fresh parsley
2 tsp wheat-free vegetable bouillon powder

1. Preheat the oven to 200C/gas mark 6. Line a baking tray with greaseproof paper.
2. Place all the ingredients in a food processor and blend for 6–8 minutes until the mixture is roughly chopped but not smooth.
3. Remove the blade from the processor, take handfuls of the mixture and shape into medium-sized balls. Place on the baking tray and press down gently with the back of a spoon to form burger shapes. You should get between 6 and 8 burgers, depending on the size of the burger.
4. Transfer to the oven and bake for 25 minutes or until golden brown in colour. Serve with a crispy green salad and Tangy Barbecue Relish (see p.224).

Risotto rice

Rice is a fantastic source of those all important B vitamins that are essential for the breakdown of proteins, fats and carbs in the body as well as being a good stress-buster.

SERVES 4
200 g risotto rice
2 tbsp wild rice
4 tsp olive oil
3 onions, peeled and diced
1 fennel bulb, trimmed, finely sliced and cored
100 ml rice milk
100 g baby corn
125 g cherry tomatoes, halved
6 tbsp chopped fresh basil

1. Mix the rices together, rinse and place in a medium-sized pan with 500 ml water. Bring to the boil, then lower the heat and simmer for 25–30 minutes until all the liquid is absorbed. The rice should be cooked but slightly firm.
2. Heat the olive oil in a medium-sized pan with 2 tablespoons of water and add the onion, fennel and rice milk. Cook for 10 minutes until the onion is soft but not coloured.
3. Stir this mixture through the rice along with the remaining ingredients and serve immediately on a bed of curly endive, baby spinach and rocket leaves.

Aduki bean stew with millet mash

If you want to lose weight this is the dish for you. As well as being great for weight loss, aduki beans also contain high levels of B vitamins to nourish the adrenal glands and iron, zinc and manganese, all of which are excellent for general health. They strengthen the body's energy battery, the spleen, and soak up damp in the body like a sponge.

SERVES 4

200 g aduki beans, presoaked for 12 hours or overnight in cold water
1 wheat-free vegetable stock cube
1 onion, peeled and finely chopped
2 carrots, trimmed, peeled and thickly sliced
1 leek, washed, trimmed and finely sliced
half a butternut squash, peeled, halved, deseeded and cut into chunky pieces
half teaspoon ground cumin
half teaspoon turmeric powder
250 g curly kale
4 tbsp chopped fresh chervil

1. Drain the beans and rinse well. Place in a large saucepan of water and bring to the boil. Boil hard for 15 minutes to remove the toxins. Drain and rinse well.
2. Return the beans to the pan with a litre of fresh cold water. Add the stock cube and bring to the boil. Lower the heat and simmer for 10 minutes. Add the vegetables, cumin and turmeric and simmer for a further 10–15 minutes.
3. Add the kale and cook for a few minutes until just tender. Sprinkle with chervil and serve with Millet Mash (see p.158) and Onion Gravy (see p.221).

Main meals

157

Millet mash

If you are a potato addict and are missing your buttery and milky mashed white potatoes, then this dish is going to make your day. Too many white potatoes in your diet can have an acidifying effect on your body, due to the fast energy glucose release that they cause. Millet, by contrast, supports the digestive organs, helps to improve nutrient uptake and aids in the removal of unwanted excess acid from years of poor eating. To top it all, it also helps to inhibit the growth of fungus and nasty bacteria.

SERVES 4
100 g millet
1 pinch of sea salt
1 onion, peeled and finely chopped
1 cauliflower, cut into small florets

1. Wash the millet and drain well. Place in a medium-sized pan of water, add the salt and bring to the boil. Lower the heat and simmer for 20 minutes.
2. Place the onion in a medium-sized pan with the cauliflower and enough water to cover. Bring to the boil, then lower the heat and simmer for 4–5 minutes. Remove from the heat, drain and return to the pan. Mash with a potato masher.
3. Drain the millet and mix through the mashed cauliflower and onion mixture. Serve warm.

Cherry tomato and artichoke pasta with avocado dressing

I want to take the opportunity here today to tell you to stop eating processed, white pasta. Instead, check out green pastas made from spinach, brown pastas made from spelt grain and even yellow corn or rice pasta and quinoa pasta. You can find all kinds of varieties in your local health food shop. In this dish, I use an ingredient called umeboshi paste which is a fantastic way of flavouring a dish. It's a superb digestive tonic.

SERVES 4

250 g wheat-free pasta
125 g marinated artichokes
125 g cherry tomatoes, halved
4 tbsp chopped fresh basil, plus extra to garnish

AVOCADO DRESSING:

2 avocados, halved and stoned
juice of 1 lemon
1 garlic clove, peeled and chopped
1 tbsp white miso paste
1 tsp umeboshi paste
1 tbsp olive oil

1. Bring a medium-sized pan of water to the boil, add the pasta and cook for 3–4 minutes until al dente (just cooked); it will not take long so don't overcook it. Drain and rinse well under cold water.

2. To make the dressing, scoop the flesh from the avocados into a small food processor bowl. Add all the other dressing ingredients and blend until smooth. If necessary add a little cold water in order to form a smooth paste.

3. Mix together the pasta, artichokes, tomatoes and the chopped basil.

4. Serve with the avocado dressing drizzled over the top, garnished with the extra basil.

Main meals

Aubergine and chickpea tagine

A tagine is a Moroccan casserole dish designed to maximize flavour and retain nutrients. If you don't have a tagine then a normal casserole dish will do fine.

SERVES 4

1 tbsp olive oil
2 onions, peeled and chopped
2 celery stalks, trimmed and sliced
1 small leek, washed, trimmed and sliced
2 garlic cloves, peeled and finely chopped
half teaspoon ground cumin
half teaspoon coriander
half teaspoon cinnamon
400-g can chopped organic tomatoes
1 large aubergine, diced into 2-cm pieces
2 small red peppers, deseeded and diced
2 small yellow peppers, deseeded and diced
1 tbsp wheat-free vegetable bouillon powder
410-g can chickpeas, drained and rinsed
1 handful fresh basil leaves
1 handful fresh coriander leaves

1. Place the oil in a tagine or covered casserole dish and warm gently over a low heat. Add the onions, celery, leek and garlic and cook for 2 minutes. Add all the spices, tomatoes and vegetables and cook for a further 3 minutes.

2. Mix the bouillon with 2 tablespoons of boiling water and add to the tagine.

3. Lower the heat and simmer for 40–50 minutes.

4. Add the chickpeas and cook for a further 5 minutes.

5. Add the fresh herbs and serve from the tagine or casserole dish with brown rice.

Rice vegetable paella

Most people I meet are so deficient in B vitamins that it shocks me. Low energy, weight issues and many other niggly health complaints often result. Enter rice to the rescue. Brown rice is loaded with B vitamins and incredibly easy to prepare.

SERVES 4
100 g long-grain brown rice
sea salt
2 tsp olive oil
2 onions, peeled and diced
2 celery stalks, trimmed and finely sliced
2 carrots, trimmed, peeled and finely sliced
6 cauliflower florets
half teaspoon turmeric powder
few strands of saffron
1 courgette, trimmed and finely sliced
half a red pepper, deseeded and finely sliced
50 g fresh garden peas
2 tbsp chopped fresh parsley

1. Place the rice in a medium-sized saucepan with 250 ml slightly salted water. Bring to the boil, then lower the heat and simmer for 20–25 minutes until the liquid is absorbed. The rice should be cooked but slightly firm. Remove from the heat and allow to stand for 10 minutes.

2. Place the oil in a saucepan with a little water. Add the onions, celery and carrot and cook for a few minutes to soften but not colour the vegetables.

3. Add the cauliflower, turmeric and saffron and cook for 5 minutes. Add the courgettes and pepper, cook for a further 2 minutes, then stir in the rice. Sprinkle over the peas and parsley and serve.

Main meals

Shiitake mushroom risotto

Barley has a sweet flavour and is particularly good for indigestion, oedema or dry skin. It does contain gluten, a substance to which some people are sensitive, but in very low levels.

SERVES 4
2 tbsp olive oil
1 large onion, peeled and chopped
2 garlic cloves, peeled and finely chopped
150 g pot barley, rinsed and drained
1 wheat-free vegetable stock cube
120 g shiitake mushrooms, trimmed and finely sliced
2 tbsp chopped fresh parsley

1. Heat 1 tablespoon of olive oil and 1 tablespoon of water in a medium-sized pan. Add the onion and garlic and cook over a low heat until soft but not coloured.

2. Stir in the barley, add 1.5 litres cold water and the stock cube. Bring to the boil, then lower the heat and allow to simmer for about 10 minutes until the barley is tender and all the liquid has been absorbed.

3. Heat the remaining olive oil in a small pan and sauté the mushrooms for 2–3 minutes. Stir into the risotto mixture with the freshly chopped parsley and serve.

Hearty lentil stew

This dish is a superb way to strengthen the nervous system. When stressed, the kidneys take a beating and the adrenals pump out too many stress hormones, depleting the body of much-needed vitamin B. It's also a good transitional dish as it contains a few white potatoes. If you're on a weight loss programme then simply leave them out.

The key to maintaining the flavour is not to overcook the lentils. You'll know this has happened if they start to break up.

SERVES 4

225 g brown lentils
2 onions, peeled and finely chopped
1 wheat-free vegetable stock cube
4 carrots, trimmed, peeled and chopped
half a butternut squash, peeled, deseeded and chopped
1 sweet potato, peeled and diced
4 small white potatoes, peeled and diced
1 celery stalk, trimmed and chopped
50 g fresh garden peas
100 g fresh watercress
2 tbsp chopped fresh dill
1 tsp tamari sauce

1. Soak the lentils in cold water for 20 minutes. Rinse thoroughly and drain.

2. Place the onions and vegetable stock cube in a saucepan with 750 ml water and bring to the boil. Add the lentils, carrots, squash, sweet potato and white potatoes. Bring back to the boil, then lower the heat and simmer for 10 minutes. Add the celery and simmer for a further 5 minutes.

3. Add the peas, watercress, dill and tamari and serve with salt-free sauerkraut.

To turn this into a soup for the next day, add more water, extra fresh herbs of your choice, some more stock and blend until smooth. Fabulous.

Main meals

Vegetable sushi rolls

This is one of the best dishes to get your children involved
in the kitchen. Children eating seaweed? They love it. In fact,
nori is my favourite sea veggie because of its high nutrient
vitamin and mineral content. Nori is also a great source of
protein and the most easily digested of all the sea vegetables.
If you are prone to colds, have high blood pressure, catarrh,
water retention or lack of energy, this is your dish.

SERVES 4–6
200 g brown rice
1 wheat-free vegetable stock cube
17 g nori sushi sheets
2 avocados, flesh mashed with squeeze
of lime or lemon juice
half a cucumber, peeled and cut into julienne
(matchstick) strips
half a small white cabbage, shredded
1 large carrot, trimmed, peeled and grated
100 g alfalfa sprouts
1 small red onion, peeled and finely chopped
1 red pepper, deseeded and finely shredded
1 tbsp pickled ginger or sushi daikon

1. Place the rice and stock cube in a small saucepan and add
500 ml of boiling water. Bring back to the boil, cover, lower
the heat and simmer for 7–10 minutes or until the water has
been absorbed.

2. Place a sushi sheet on a flat surface or on a bamboo mat,
if you have one. Spread evenly with the mashed avocado,
leaving 2.5 cm of the sheet uncovered at the far end. Spread
with a thin layer of rice.

3. Arrange a row of each remaining ingredient in the centre
of the roll. Carefully fold the edge of the sheet closest to you
over the filling. Tuck the end in and begin to roll, as tightly
as possible. Before you reach the end, moisten the top edge
of the nori sheet with a little water so that it sticks. Wrap
in cling film and place in the fridge until required.

4. Repeat with the remaining sheets.

5. To serve slice the sushi with a very sharp knife into 2-cm pieces. Serve with a little tamari sauce to dip.

Top tip

Don't make the nori rolls too thick – they need to be eaten in one bite. Find the ideal proportions. But if you are involving the kids, let them have fun – that's the whole point of this dish! Eventually, you will become an expert sushi roller, and so will your kids.

Mushroom stroganoff

My favourite mushrooms are shiitake, for their immune system boosting properties. If you suffer from thrush or yeast conditions then stay away from mushrooms, with the exception of shiitakes.

SERVES 4
1 red onion, peeled and finely sliced
2 tsp olive oil
1 garlic clove, peeled and finely chopped
125 g shiitake mushrooms, trimmed
4 large Portobello mushrooms, trimmed and thickly sliced
125 g chestnut mushrooms, some sliced, some whole
150 ml soya milk
3 tbsp chopped fresh flat leaf parsley

1. Place the onion in a medium-sized frying pan with the olive oil and 1 tablespoon of water and cook gently for 2–3 minutes. Add the garlic and mushrooms and cook for a further 3–4 minutes.
2. Add the soya milk and cook for a further 5 minutes on a medium heat. Sprinkle on the parsley and serve with Gourmet Brown Rice (see p.185).

Tempeh autumn stew

Tempeh is compressed soybeans and can be bought in
a health food shop fresh, frozen, precooked or dried. It's
an excellent meat substitute, is high in omega 3 'good' fats
and the energy vitamin, B12. I use pumpkin in this dish as
it's helpful for regulating blood sugar levels. If you have
diabetes, suffer from hypoglycaemia (blood sugar swings),
or get shaky if you don't eat at regular intervals, then this
dish could help.

SERVES 4
6–9 whole baby onions, peeled
2 tbsp olive oil
225-g block tempeh
1 strip kombu sea vegetable
3 carrots, trimmed, peeled and cut into chunks
2.5-cm piece fresh root ginger, peeled and sliced
2 sprigs fresh rosemary
1 tbsp wheat-free vegetable bouillon powder
4 sprigs fresh thyme
quarter of a small pumpkin, peeled and cut into large pieces
125 g fresh garden peas
2 tsp mugi miso
2 tbsp chopped fresh parsley

1. Place the onions and oil in a medium-sized casserole dish.
Add enough water to cover them and boil for 2–3 minutes.
2. Add the tempeh, kombu, carrot, ginger, rosemary, bouillon
powder and thyme. Add more water to cover the vegetables.
Cover and bring to the boil, then lower the heat and simmer
uncovered for 10 minutes.
3. Add the pumpkin and simmer for a further 10 minutes.
4. Blanch the peas in boiling water for 2–3 minutes. Drain
and refresh in cold water.
5. Take 2 tablespoons of juice from the casserole dish and
mix with the mugi miso and return to the pan. Serve with
the peas and garnished with the parsley.

Main meals

167

Tempeh with sweet and sour red cabbage

Cabbage strengthens the liver and contains anti-cancer nutrients, so don't skimp on it.

SERVES 4
225-g block tempeh
1 strip kombu sea vegetable
2 tsp tamari sauce
4 onions, peeled and finely sliced
2 bay leaves
half a red cabbage, finely shredded
sea salt
1 tsp mixed spice
half teaspoon freshly grated nutmeg
3 tbsp rice vinegar
3 tbsp freshly pressed apple juice
1 tbsp olive oil
1 dessertspoonful arrowroot dissolved in 1 tbsp cold water
2 spring onions, trimmed and finely sliced
2 carrots, trimmed, peeled and finely grated

1. Cut the tempeh into 4 pieces and place in a medium-sized pan with the kombu and tamari. Half-cover the tempeh with water and bring to the boil. Lower the heat and simmer for 10 minutes, then drain. Discard the kombu.

2. Place the onions in a medium-sized casserole dish and add enough water to cover. Add the bay leaves, bring to the boil, then lower the heat and simmer for 5–7 minutes. Add the cabbage, seasonings, vinegar and apple juice and cook for a further 10–15 minutes.

3. Heat the oil in a small frying pan with 2 tablespoons of water, add the tempeh and pan-fry for a couple of minutes on each side.

4. Add the arrowroot to the red cabbage mixture.

5. Put the tempeh on top of the cabbage and serve garnished with the spring onions and grated carrot.

Tofu with steamed vegetables

SERVES 4

2 courgettes, trimmed and sliced
3 carrots, trimmed, peeled and sliced
100 g French beans, trimmed
1 head broccoli, cut into florets
1 tbsp olive oil
1 garlic clove, peeled and crushed
1 tsp tamari sauce
2 tbsp freshly pressed apple juice
225-g block smoked tofu, cut into 2-cm cubes
fresh basil and parsley

1. Steam the courgettes and carrots one at a time in an electric steamer or over a pan of boiling water. Steam the courgettes first for 3–4 minutes and then the carrots for 7–8 minutes.

2. Blanch the beans and broccoli in boiling water for 3–4 minutes, drain well and refresh in cold water.

3. Heat the oil in a medium-sized casserole pan with 1 tablespoon of water, then add the garlic and cook for 1 minute. Add all the cooked vegetables, tamari, apple juice, the tofu and herbs and cook for a further minute. Serve immediately.

Wholewheat oat pancakes with ratatouille

Oats are soothing to the body's nervous system, strengthening to the stomach and spleen and good cholesterol-busters. They have also been found to be a good friend to the sex drive. You have probably heard of the saying 'sow your wild oats'. So you can do that with my pancakes. Sometimes I also add raw sprouted seeds to the filling.

SERVES 4–6
PANCAKES:
125 g wholewheat flour
2 level tbsp oat bran
avocado oil or virgin olive oil
FILLING:
1 small onion, peeled and finely chopped
1 garlic clove, peeled and finely chopped
1 red pepper, deseeded and finely chopped
1 yellow or green pepper, deseeded and finely chopped
400 g can chopped organic tomatoes
1 aubergine, trimmed and chopped into 2-cm pieces (optional)
2 courgettes, trimmed, halved lengthways and sliced
1 tbsp wheat-free vegetable bouillon powder
410 g no salt mixed beans
4–6 sprigs fresh basil

1. Blend the flour and oat bran together with 300 ml cold water in a food processor or with a hand-held blender for 1 minute. Allow to rest while you prepare the filling.
2. Place the onion, garlic, peppers, tomatoes, aubergine and courgettes in a medium-sized pan with the bouillon powder and 1 tablespoon of hot water.
3. Cook over a medium heat for 10–15 minutes, then stir in the beans. Cook for a further 5 minutes. Remove from the heat and set aside.

4. Heat a 20-cm non-stick frying pan, drizzle with a little oil and then wipe with a piece of paper towel. Add a thin layer of batter to coat the base of the pan; tilt the pan to coat evenly.

5. Cook for 2 minutes until the sides of the pancake begin to lift. Slide a palette knife underneath and flip the pancake carefully on to the other side. Cook for a further 2 minutes until set and lightly browned.

6. Slide the pancake on to a plate and keep warm in the oven. Repeat process with the remaining mixture. Reheat the filling and spoon into the centre of the prepared pancakes. Fold over the pancake and place on warmed serving plates. Garnish with the basil sprigs.

Root vegetables and tofu en papillote

Tofu is a very good source of protein. Researchers have discovered that regular intake of soy protein can help lower too-high cholesterol levels. Tofu also contains phytoestrogens which have been shown to alleviate symptoms associated with the menopause. Tofu tends to be neutral in taste and will take on the flavour of the seasonings in a dish.

SERVES 4
2 tsp olive oil
2 carrots, trimmed, peeled and cut into fine julienne (matchstick) strips
1 parsnip, trimmed, peeled and cut into fine julienne (matchstick) strips
2 sweet potatoes, peeled and cut into fine julienne (matchstick) strips
2 courgettes, trimmed and cut into fine julienne (matchstick) strips
225-g block smoked tofu, cut into 2-cm cubes
1 tsp ground cumin
2 tsp tamari sauce
4 tsp freshly pressed apple juice
4 bay leaves
2 tbsp sesame seeds
4 tbsp fresh beansprouts

1. Preheat the oven to 200C/gas mark 6.
2. Take 4 pieces of foil, 30-cm square, and brush the centre of each with a little oil.
3. Mix all the vegetables together in a large bowl and divide between the foil sheets.

4. Place the tofu on top of the vegetables. Season with the cumin and bring the foil up around the vegetables to form a parcel. Add the tamari and apple juice and top with a bay leaf. Add a little water to each parcel and then scrunch up the foil to seal everything in.

5. Transfer to the oven and bake for 20 minutes.

6. Remove from the oven and allow to stand for 5 minutes. Transfer the foil parcels to serving plates. Open up the parcels slightly and sprinkle on the sesame seeds and sprouts and serve immediately.

Fragrant Thai vegetable curry

400-ml can coconut milk
half teaspoon ground coriander
half teaspoon ground cumin
2 kaffir lime leaves
2-cm piece fresh root ginger, peeled and sliced
2 stalks lemon grass, cut into 2-cm pieces
2 tbsp chopped fresh coriander
100 g sugar snap peas
half a red pepper, deseeded and diced
half a yellow pepper, deseeded and diced
100 g baby corn, halved lengthways
1 aubergine, trimmed and chopped
2 courgettes, trimmed and chopped
2 spring onions, trimmed and finely sliced
1 handful of beansprouts
fresh basil leaves

1. Heat the coconut milk in a wok until boiling then add the spices, lime leaves, ginger, lemon grass and coriander. Cook for 2–3 minutes on a high heat.
2. Add the peas, peppers, baby corn, aubergine and courgettes and cook for a further 3–4 minutes or until the vegetables are just cooked.
3. Sprinkle on the spring onions, beansprouts and basil and serve immediately from the wok with brown rice.

Vegetarian chilli

SERVES 4

two 410-g cans red kidney beans, drained and rinsed
260 g canned sweetcorn, drained and rinsed
two 400-g cans chopped organic tomatoes
1 onion, peeled and cut into large chunks
2 courgettes, trimmed and diced
100 g frozen broad beans
1 garlic clove, peeled and chopped
1 tsp ground cardamom
1 tsp ground cinnamon
1 tbsp tamari sauce
1 tbsp chopped fresh basil
1 handful of beansprouts
1 large beef tomato, roughly chopped
1 spring onion, trimmed and chopped

1. Preheat the oven to 180C/gas mark 4.

2. Mix all the ingredients except the spring onion and beansprouts together in a large bowl. Transfer to a large casserole dish and bake for 35–40 minutes.

3. Remove from the oven and serve garnished with the beansprouts and spring onion. Serve with brown rice.

Chickpea and tofu mild curry

SERVES 4

1 tbsp olive oil
3 onions, peeled and finely diced
sea salt
225-g block fresh tofu, cut into 2-cm cubes
410-g can chickpeas, drained and rinsed
2 tbsp chopped fresh coriander
2 carrots, trimmed, peeled and diced
1 tsp ground cumin
1 tsp ground turmeric
1 tsp ground coriander
1 tbsp mugi miso
1 tbsp arrowroot dissolved in 1 tbsp water
500 g spring greens, tough stems removed,
and roughly shredded
fresh coriander leaves

1. Heat the oil in a medium-sized pan and add the onion
and a pinch of salt. Cook gently for 10 minutes until soft
and translucent.

2. Add the tofu, chickpeas, coriander, carrots, spices and
enough water to cover. Bring to the boil, lower the heat,
cover and cook for 10 minutes.

3. Take 2 tablespoons of the cooking juices and mix
with the mugi miso and add to the stew along with the
arrowroot mixture.

4. Bring a large pan of water to the boil and cook the
spring greens for 3–4 minutes.

5. Strain and arrange on warmed serving plates. Top
with the curry, garnish with coriander leaves and serve
immediately.

Mung bean casserole

This is the best dish for ridding the body of toxins
and bacteria.

SERVES 4
250 g mung beans, presoaked for 6 hours in cold water
1 wheat-free vegetable stock cube
half teaspoon turmeric powder
half teaspoon ground cumin
3 tbsp chopped fresh coriander
1 onion, peeled and finely chopped
2 carrots, trimmed, peeled and chopped
2 endive, leaves removed
1 small bunch radishes, trimmed and halved
a few clover sprouts

1. Drain the mung beans and rinse well.
2. Bring 750 ml water to the boil and add the mung beans,
stock cube, turmeric and cumin, lower the heat and simmer
for 30 minutes. Then add the coriander, onion and carrots
and simmer for a further few minutes.
3. Arrange the endive around the edge of a deep bowl, spoon
in the casserole mixture and garnish with the radishes and
clover sprouts. Serve with brown rice and a hearty salad.

Tofu pecan stir-fry

SERVES 4

2 leeks, washed, trimmed and finely sliced
1 tsp tamari sauce
2 carrots, trimmed, peeled and cut into fine julienne
(matchstick) strips
225-g block smoked tofu, cut into 2-cm cubes
100 g baby corn, halved lengthways
3 celery stalks, trimmed and sliced
3–4 tbsp chopped pecans
1 tsp sesame oil
1 tsp orange rind

1. Heat a large wok, add a little water and then the leeks and tamari. Stir-fry for a few minutes and then add the carrots, tofu and sweetcorn. Cook for a further 5 minutes.
2. Add the celery, pecans, sesame oil and orange rind. Serve immediately on a bed of salad leaves.

Aromatic poached chicken

SERVES 4

4 skinless organic chicken breasts
1 wheat-free vegetable stock cube
1 stalk lemon grass, cut into 2-cm pieces
2 kaffir lime leaves
2-cm piece fresh root ginger, peeled and finely sliced
2 celery stalks, trimmed and sliced
1 leek, washed, trimmed and finely sliced
100 g shiitake mushrooms
1 bunch watercress, trimmed
100 g beansprouts
3 tbsp chopped fresh coriander

1. Place the chicken breasts in a medium-sized pan of water with the stock cube, lemon grass, lime leaves and ginger and bring to the boil.

2. Add the celery and leek, lower the heat and simmer for 20 minutes.

3. Add the mushrooms and cook for a further 2 minutes.

4. Remove from the heat. Take out the chicken breasts and diagonally slice.

5. Add the watercress, beansprouts and coriander to the pan.

6. Divide between 4 soup bowls, top with the sliced chicken breast and serve.

NINE
QUICK BITES

Too busy to eat healthily? I hear this all the time, but I urge you not to fall into the trap of the quick-fix, boil in the bag, processed, junk food lifestyle. 'Convenience' is a misnomer for these foods. It's not so convenient to feel tired or unwell, live with headaches, bloating, gas or weight problems. All rise for my extra quick bites. If you are on a weight-loss programme or suffer from bloating then avoid the pasta recipes.

Poached chicken with vegetables

SERVES 2
1 organic skinless chicken breast
1 tsp organic wheat-free vegetable bouillon powder
2 carrots, trimmed, peeled and sliced
1 leek, washed, trimmed and sliced
50 g fresh or frozen peas
1 tsp cornflour
1 tsp chopped fresh parsley

1. Cut the chicken breast into chunky pieces and place in a saucepan with 500 ml water and the vegetable bouillon powder. Add the carrot and leek and bring to the boil. Lower the heat and simmer for 5 minutes then add the peas. Return to the boil and simmer for 2 more minutes until the chicken is cooked.

2. Blend the cornflour with 1 tablespoon of cold water and stir into the chicken mixture. Cook for a few seconds until the cooking liquor has thickened.

3. Stir through some fresh chopped parsley and serve immediately with lightly cooked cabbage.

Baked aubergine and mushroom stack

SERVES 4
1 large aubergine, trimmed and cut lengthways into
1.5 cm slices
1 fennel bulb, trimmed and sliced
1 red onion, peeled and finely sliced
4 large flat mushrooms, trimmed
1 tbsp olive oil
4 garlic cloves, peeled and chopped

1. Preheat the oven to 200C/gas mark 6.
2. Arrange the vegetables on a large baking sheet and
glaze the aubergine, fennel slices and onion with olive oil
using a pastry brush.
3. Scatter the garlic over the vegetables.
4. Bake for 8–10 minutes or until lightly coloured.
5. Arrange the aubergine on 4 warm serving plates, top with
the fennel, then the onion and finally the whole mushrooms.
Serve immediately with a green salad.

BBQ fish kebabs

SERVES 2
300 g firm white fish such as monkfish,
cut into chunks
1 red onion, peeled and quartered
4 cherry tomatoes
1 yellow pepper, deseeded and cut into 3-cm squares
1 courgette, trimmed and cut into chunks
SAUCE:
1 red pepper, halved and deseeded
4 tomatoes, halved
2 tsp olive oil
1 tsp paprika
2 tbsp chopped fresh basil

1. If not using a barbecue, preheat the oven to 200C/
gas mark 6.
2. To make the sauce, place the pepper and tomatoes on
a baking tray, cutside up, drizzle with olive oil and roast
for 10 minutes. Allow to cool slightly then tip into a food
processor. Add the paprika and basil and blend until
smooth. Transfer to a serving bowl.
3. Thread the fish alternately with the vegetables on
to 4 large skewers. Cook for 3–4 minutes each side on a
preheated barbecue. Alternatively, bake in the preheated
oven for 7–10 minutes. Serve immediately with the sauce
on the side.

Stuffed courgettes

SERVES 2
2 large courgettes, halved lengthways
and flesh removed with a teaspoon
8 cherry tomatoes, halved
12 black pitted olives
100 g goat's cheese, crumbled
1 tsp olive oil
12 fresh basil leaves, roughly torn

1. Preheat the oven to 200C/gas mark 6.
2. Line a baking tray with aluminium foil and place the courgette boats on the foil. Arrange the cherry tomatoes, olives and goat's cheese alternately in the courgettes. Drizzle with a little olive oil, sprinkle over half the basil leaves.
3. Bake for 20 minutes and serve immediately, garnished with the rest of the basil leaves.

Gourmet brown rice

SERVES 1–2
100 g brown rice
1 wheat-free vegetable stock cube or 2 tsp miso paste
2 carrots, trimmed, peeled and finely sliced
1 celery stalk, trimmed and finely sliced

1. Place the rice in a small saucepan with 200 ml water, add the stock cube or miso and the vegetables.
2. Bring to the boil, then lower the heat and simmer for 20 minutes until the rice is tender, but not all the liquid is absorbed. Turn off the heat and allow to stand for 10 minutes before serving.

Quick bites

Pasta with roasted cherry tomatoes

I am not an advocate of eating pasta every single day.
Make it once in a while and try out green pastas and
wheat-free variations.

SERVES 2
200 g wheat-free pasta
250 g cherry tomatoes, halved
2 tsp olive oil
4 tbsp chopped fresh basil
100 g pine nuts
balsamic vinegar to dress

1. Preheat the oven to 200C/gas mark 6.
2. Place the pine nuts in a small pan over a low heat and
toast, stirring frequently until golden in colour. Set aside.
3. Bring a medium-sized pan of water to the boil, add the
pasta and cook for 3–4 minutes, or until al dente.
4. Meanwhile, place the cherry tomatoes on a baking sheet
and drizzle with a little olive oil. Roast for 4–5 minutes.
5. Drain the pasta, then toss with the tomatoes and their
juices, the basil and toasted pine nuts. Drizzle with balsamic
vinegar and serve.

Griddled peppers with cannellini beans and black olives

SERVES 2

4 mixed peppers, halved and deseeded
olive oil, to brush
410-g can cannellini beans, drained and rinsed
50 g drained weight pitted black olives
1 garlic clove, peeled and chopped
2 tbsp chopped fresh parsley
2 tsp olive oil

1. Brush the skin side of the peppers with olive oil. Heat a griddle pan until very hot then place the peppers skin side down on the griddle. Cook until the skin is beginning to wrinkle, then remove from the heat and allow to cool.
2. Place the beans, olives, garlic and parsley in a medium-sized bowl. Add the olive oil and mix well.
3. Cut the peppers into thick slices, add to the beans and serve.

Pasta salad

SERVES 2
150 g wheat-free pasta
1 courgette, trimmed and cut into
julienne (matchstick) strips
1 red pepper, deseeded and finely sliced
1 yellow pepper, deseeded and finely sliced
40 g canned sweetcorn, drained and rinsed
2 spring onions, trimmed and finely chopped
2 tbsp chopped fresh dill
2 tbsp capers (optional)

1. Bring a medium-sized pan of water to the boil, add the pasta and cook for 2–3 minutes or until al dente (just cooked). Drain and refresh in cold water. Drain well and place in a salad bowl.
2. Place a little water in a medium-sized pan and cook the courgette for 2–3 minutes. Add the peppers, mix well and remove from the heat. Toss the courgette and peppers into the cooked pasta along with all the other ingredients.
3. Just before serving toss through some Sesame Miso Dressing (see p.221).

Buckwheat salad

SERVES 2

100 g buckwheat groats
half a red pepper, deseeded and finely chopped
2 carrots, trimmed, peeled and finely diced
2 onions, peeled and finely chopped
1 bay leaf
2 tbsp diced pickled gherkins
2 tsp chopped fresh dill
2 spring onions, trimmed and finely chopped

DRESSING:

1 tbsp peanut butter
1 tbsp Dijon mustard
1 tsp white miso paste
1 tbsp freshly pressed apple juice

1. Rinse the buckwheat and drain. Place in a
medium-sized saucepan.
2. Add the pepper, carrots, onions, bay leaf and enough
water to cover.
3. Bring to the boil, then lower the heat and simmer
for 15–20 minutes. All liquid should be reduced; drain
if necessary.
4. Mix in the gherkin, dill and spring onions.
5. Mix the dressing ingredients with 2 tablespoons
of hot water, drizzle over the salad and serve.

Quick tofu

SERVES 2
1 tbsp olive oil
2 onions, peeled and finely chopped
50 g canned sweetcorn, drained and rinsed
100 g shiitake mushrooms, trimmed
juice of half a lemon
half teaspoon turmeric powder
225-g block tofu
100-g block smoked tofu
1 bunch watercress
2 tbsp pine nuts

1. In a medium-sized pan heat the oil and the onion with
2 tablespoons of water. Cook for 10 minutes until soft but
not coloured.
2. Add the sweetcorn, mushrooms, lemon juice and turmeric
and stir. Crumble in the tofu. Cook for a further 10 minutes.
3. Mix in the watercress and pine nuts and serve.

Quick lentil stew with artichokes

SERVES 2

200 g Puy lentils
1 onion, peeled and sliced
4 celery stalks, trimmed and sliced
4 carrots, trimmed, peeled and sliced
3 parsnips, trimmed, peeled and sliced
400-g can artichoke hearts
1 leek, washed, trimmed and sliced
1 wheat-free vegetable stock cube
300 g kale leaves
2 tbsp chopped fresh parsley or chervil

1. Rinse the Puy lentils and drain. Place in a large pan with all the other ingredients except the kale and herbs.
2. Add enough water to cover, bring to the boil, then lower the heat and simmer for 20 minutes.
3. Remove from the heat, mix in the kale leaves to warm through. Sprinkle on the herbs and serve.

Tuna steaks with black-eye pea salsa

SERVES 2
two 120-g tuna steak
200 g fresh rocket
200 g fresh watercress
SALSA:
410-g can black-eye peas, drained and rinsed
1 red onion, peeled and finely diced
1 red pepper, deseeded and finely diced
1 beef tomato, halved, deseeded and finely chopped
2 tbsp chopped fresh coriander
2 tsp olive oil or hemp oil

1. Heat a griddle pan until very hot. Sear the tuna for
2 minutes, then turn and cook the other side for 2–3 minutes.
Remove from the heat and allow to cool.

2. To make the salsa, mix together the peas with the onion,
pepper, tomato, coriander and oil.

3. Arrange the rocket and watercress on a plate.

4. Place the tuna on the salad, spoon the salsa over the
top and serve immediately.

Stir-fry vegetables with arame

Don't be put off by the brown, stringy appearance of the
seaweed arame. Arame is a source of calcium and iron.
It is supportive for the spleen, pancreas and stomach
and delicious in this recipe.

SERVES 2
50 g arame sea vegetable
10 baby corn
1 onion, peeled and sliced
2 tsp olive oil
2 carrots, trimmed, peeled and cut into julienne
(matchstick) strips
1 bunch asparagus, cut into bite-sized pieces
1 red pepper, deseeded and finely sliced
1 fennel bulb, trimmed, cored and finely sliced
zest of half a lemon
1-cm piece root ginger, peeled and grated
1 tbsp chopped fresh coriander
1 tbsp chopped fresh chervil

1. Soak the arame in cold water for 10 minutes and drain well.
Blanch the corn in boiling water for 2–3 minutes. Drain and
refresh in cold water.

2. Place the onion, olive oil and 2 tablespoons of water in
a wok and cook for 5–7 minutes until soft.

3. Add the arame, corn and all the other ingredients, except
the coriander and chervil, and cook for 2–3 minutes. Serve
immediately, garnished with the coriander and chervil.

Quick bites

TEN
SNACKS

I want you to change your entire consciousness about snacking. From this day forward, your mental association with the word 'snack' will be transformed. You will no longer associate the word 'snack' with junk foods like crisps, biscuits, ice cream, pork rinds, cakes and sweets. When you now hear the word 'snack', you will think of healthy wholesome goodies, simple yet amazing foods such as vegetable sticks, fruits, raw nuts, hemp seeds, sunflower seeds and a whole host of others. You can make the leap. I did it years ago, and I would not expect you to do something that I haven't done myself. It will make a huge difference to your life.

Crunchy kale

This can be eaten as a snack or sprinkled over pasta, risotto or salads.

SERVES 4
olive oil
100 g curly kale, stems removed
1 tsp dried mixed herbs

1. Preheat the oven to 180C/gas mark 4. Line a baking tray with foil and lightly brush with a little olive oil using a pastry brush.
2. Cut the leaves into wide slices and arrange evenly spaced on the baking tray.
3. Bake for 15–20 minutes, being sure to stir them at least twice while they're baking. The kale leaves are ready when they're bright green and crisp.
4. Remove the leaves from the oven and season with dried mixed herbs. Eat on the same day.

Sesame rice balls

This is also delicious served cold. Umeboshi is an easy-to-digest vegetable protein snack. It has an alkalizing effect on the body, which is good for people who have eaten excess amounts of red meat (one too many burgers and chips!).

MAKES ABOUT 12
200 g brown rice
8 tbsp sesame seeds
410-g can red kidney beans, drained and rinsed
2 tsp umeboshi paste
4 tbsp lemon juice
tamari sauce, for dipping

1. Preheat the oven to 180C/gas mark 4. Line a baking tray with greaseproof paper.
2. Bring a large pan of water to the boil. Add the rice and cook for 20 minutes. Drain and rinse in cold water.
3. Heat the sesame seeds in a medium-sized pan over a moderate heat until lightly toasted.
4. Place the rice, beans, umeboshi and lemon juice in a food processor and blend until it forms a stiff mixture.
5. Roll the rice mixture into walnut-sized balls, then roll in the sesame seeds and place on the prepared baking tray.
6. Bake for 12–15 minutes until hot and serve with the tamari as a dipping sauce.

Sesame squash spread

MAKES 100–150 ML
KEEPS FOR TWO DAYS IN THE FRIDGE OR
ONE MONTH IN THE FREEZER
500 g butternut squash, peeled, deseeded and cut into
2.5-cm pieces
5 tbsp sesame seeds
1 tsp brown miso paste
1 pinch cinnamon

1. Place the squash in a medium-sized saucepan and
cover with water. Bring to the boil, then lower the heat and
simmer for 10–15 minutes until tender when pierced with
a knife. Drain well and blend in a food processor or with
a hand-held blender.
2. Heat the sesame seeds in a small pan until lightly
toasted and add to the purée with the miso and cinnamon.
3. Blend until smooth, adding a little water if necessary.
4. Transfer to a small bowl and cover. Place in the fridge
until required.

Top tip
My spreads are very versatile. Add to salads for extra
flavour; use as dips for veggie crudités and spread on my
Squash Bread (see p.207) for a delicious snack any time
of the day.

Ginger squash butter

MAKES 100–150 ML
KEEPS FOR TWO DAYS IN THE FRIDGE OR
ONE MONTH IN THE FREEZER
**600 g butternut squash, peeled, deseeded and cut into
2.5-cm pieces
1 tbsp miso paste
2-cm piece fresh root ginger, finely grated
zest of half a lemon**

1. Place the squash in a medium-sized pan and cover
with cold water.

2. Bring to the boil, then lower the heat and simmer
for 10–15 minutes until tender when pierced with a knife.
Drain well and return to the pan.

3. Add the miso, ginger and lemon zest and mash with
a potato masher until smooth. Transfer to a small bowl,
cover and place in the fridge until required.

Butter bean spread

MAKES 100–150 ML
KEEPS FOR TWO DAYS IN THE FRIDGE
410-g can butter beans, drained and rinsed
2 garlic cloves, peeled and crushed
2 tsp olive oil
1 handful fresh parsley

1. Place all the ingredients in a food processor and blend until smooth.
2. Transfer to a bowl, cover and chill until required.

Sweet carrot butter

MAKES 100–150 ML
KEEPS FOR TWO DAYS IN THE FRIDGE OR
ONE MONTH IN THE FREEZER
450g carrots, trimmed, peeled and sliced
1 tbsp tahini
2 tsp arrowroot mixed with 1 tbsp cold water

1. Place the carrots in a medium-sized saucepan and cover with water. Bring to the boil, then lower the heat and simmer for 10–15 minutes until tender when pierced with a knife. Drain well.
2. Blend the carrots in a food processor or with a hand-held blender and return to the saucepan.
3. Add the tahini and arrowroot and cook for 1–2 minutes until thick.
4. Transfer to a bowl and cover and chill until required.

Cashew butter

MAKES 75-100 ML
KEEPS FOR THREE DAYS IN THE FRIDGE
200 g cashews, presoaked in water overnight
1 tsp tamari sauce

1. Drain the cashews and then place in a food processor
with the tamari and 2 tablespoons of water. Blend until
smooth; you may need to scrape down the sides during
the processing.
2. Transfer to a small bowl, cover and place in the fridge
until required.

Almond paté

MAKES 75-100 ML
KEEPS FOR THREE DAYS IN THE FRIDGE
200 g whole almonds, presoaked in water overnight
75 g pine nuts
2 tbsp lemon juice
2 tbsp olive oil
1 clove garlic, peeled and crushed
3 tbsp chopped fresh basil

1. Drain the almonds and then place in a food processor
with all the other ingredients and 2 tablespoons of water.
Blend until smooth; you may need to scrape down the
sides during the processing.
2. Transfer to a small bowl, cover and place in the fridge
until required.

Asparagus spread

MAKES 100 ML
1 bunch asparagus trimmings (tips reserved for a salad)
1 handful fresh herbs such as coriander or chervil
1 small onion, peeled and roughly chopped
2 tsp miso paste

1. Steam the asparagus for 3–4 minutes.
2. Place all the ingredients in a food processor and
blend until smooth.
3. Transfer to a bowl and eat on the same day.

Parsnip spread

MAKES 150 ML
KEEPS FOR ONE DAY IN THE FRIDGE
3 parsnips, trimmed, peeled and chopped
2 carrots, trimmed, peeled and chopped
2 tbsp tahini
2 tsp tamari sauce

1. Place the parsnips and carrots in a medium-sized pan
and cover with water. Bring to the boil, then lower the heat
and simmer for 10–15 minutes until tender when pierced
with a knife. Drain well.
2. Place in a food processor and blend until smooth. Add
the other ingredients and process for a further 30 seconds.
3. Transfer to a small bowl, cover and place in the fridge
until required.

Black olive tapenade

MAKES 125 ML
KEEPS FOR FIVE DAYS IN THE FRIDGE
100 g drained pitted black olives
2 garlic cloves, peeled and crushed
1 tsp lemon juice

1. Blend all the ingredients in a food processor until smooth.
2. Transfer to a clean screw-top jar and place in the fridge until required.

Guacamole dip

MAKES 125 ML
2 large ripe avocados, stoned, peeled and chopped
2 spring onions, trimmed and chopped
1 garlic clove, peeled and crushed
1 tbsp chopped fresh coriander
juice of 2 limes

Place all the ingredients in a food processor and blend until smooth. Eat on the same day.

Raw salsa

MAKES 175 ML
KEEPS FOR THREE DAYS IN THE FRIDGE
200 g cherry tomatoes, quartered
4 spring onions, trimmed and finely chopped
1 garlic clove, peeled and chopped
400-g can black-eye peas, drained and rinsed
juice of 1 lemon
2 tbsp chopped fresh coriander

Mix all the ingredients together, cover and chill
until required.

Tahini salsa

MAKES 175 ML
2 beef tomatoes, deseeded and finely chopped
1 yellow pepper, deseeded and finely chopped
1 red onion, peeled and finely chopped
juice of 1 lime
1 tbsp tahini
2 tbsp sesame seeds

1. Mix the tomatoes, pepper and onion together in a
medium-sized bowl. Add the lime juice and tahini and
stir well.
2. Sprinkle with the sesame seeds and eat on the
same day.

Home-made houmous

MAKES 200 ML
KEEPS FOR TWO DAYS IN THE FRIDGE
410-g can chickpeas, drained and rinsed
1 garlic clove, peeled and crushed
3 tbsp tahini
juice of half a lemon
2 tbsp chopped fresh coriander
1 tbsp olive oil

1. Place all the ingredients in a food processor and blend until smooth.
2. Transfer to a small bowl, cover and chill until required.

Pickle relish

MAKES 125 ML
KEEPS FOR FIVE DAYS IN THE FRIDGE
1 onion, peeled and finely chopped
1 green pepper, deseeded and diced
1 red pepper, deseeded and diced
100 g cherry tomatoes, halved
2 tbsp cider vinegar
1 tsp barley malt syrup

1. Place all the ingredients in a medium-sized saucepan and cook very slowly over a gentle heat for 40–45 minutes. Add a little water as required.
2. Transfer to a clean screw-top jar and allow to cool. Place in the fridge and chill until required.

Sweet potato wedges

2 sweet potatoes, cut into chunky chips
1 tbsp olive oil

1. Preheat the oven to 200C/gas mark 6.

2. Bring a large pan of water to the boil, add the sweet potato and blanch for 4–5 minutes.

3. Drain the potato and return to the pan. Toss well with the olive oil and transfer to a baking tray.

4. Cook for 25–30 minutes and serve with Guacamole Dip (see p.203) and Raw Salsa (see p.203).

Top tip

You can also bake beetroot, squash, pumpkin and parsnips in the oven for approximately 25 minutes for really easy and delicious snacks.

Gluten-free squash bread

1 small butternut squash
300g gluten-free flour
2 tsp baking powder
1 tsp herbal seasoning (optional)
2 tbsp olive oil

1. Preheat the oven to 200C/gas mark 6.

2. Place the whole butternut squash on a baking tray and bake for 45 minutes or until very soft. Cool on the tray for 30 minutes.

3. Carefully peel the skin from the squash and cut away the stalk. Transfer to a large bowl and break open using a spoon. Scoop out and discard any seeds. Mash well with a potato masher. Measure out 375 g and place in a large bowl.

4. Add the flour, baking powder and seasoning, if using. Stir in 65 ml cold water and the olive oil and mix together with a large spoon. Place on a lightly floured surface and knead until soft and spongy. Add a little more flour if the mixture is too sticky. Form into a round loaf 12 cm in diameter.

5. Place on a lightly oiled baking tray and make a cross on the top with a sharp knife. Bake in the oven for 30–35 minutes.

6. Remove from the oven and using oven gloves carefully turn the bread over and tap the base gently. It should sound hollow. If it doesn't, return to the oven and cook for a further 5 minutes. Serve the bread warm or cold.

MY TOP SNACK FOODS

Here's my list of top snack foods, ranging from fruit and veg to sea vegetables and (my all-time favourites) raw nuts and seeds. They're all easily available. Buy organic where possible, and only buy nuts and seeds that are salt- and sugar-free.

» **Dates: The Anti-Stress Snack** These dried fruits are great for helping to relax the body. As with fresh fruit, buy organic where possible.

» **Fruit** This literally means any piece of fresh fruit.

» **Hemp Seeds** Hemp seeds have a smooth nutty flavour and make delicious snacks. The raw shelled ones taste best. Eat them on their own or mixed into avocados, sweet potatoes or salads. Hemp seeds are absolutely exceptional sources of EFAs and zinc. If you want to feel sexy, then this is the seed for you!

» **Nuts** One of my staple snacks. Try Brazil, the good mood nut, hazelnuts (my favourite), almonds or, in fact, any nut of your choice. You don't need a lot; a few, or a handful, is just right. Nuts are delicious raw but you can also soak or steam them.

Soaked Nuts Soaking raw nuts in water overnight is a good way of enjoying them and makes them easy to digest.

Steamed Nuts When you steam nuts (and some seeds too), it gives them a completely different texture and flavour. As an added benefit, nuts that are steamed, as opposed to raw can be easier to digest. Try steaming cashews or almonds for a completely new taste experience!

» **Pumpkin Seeds** A fantastic source of zinc and EFAs to boost your sex drive. So, don't miss out on them. Try steaming them with soy sauce – fantastic!

» **Sauerkraut** I will let you in on a little secret: my patients love sauerkraut for its ability to increase their sex drive! Try a couple of cupfuls a day to get you started.

» **Soaked Chickpeas** This is one of my favourite snacks. I like to soak them overnight and eat them raw in the morning. Leave them for long enough, and they'll start to sprout, maximizing nutrient content and digestibility.

» **Sprouts** Aduki, alfafa, clover, fenugreek, green peas, lentils, mung, quinoa, radish, broccoli seeds, sunflower seeds or millet.

» **Sunflower Seeds** My 'pick me up' choice in the middle of the day.

» **Toasted Nori Strips** You can buy these from a health food shop or bake them in the oven yourself. My kids love to eat these instead of crisps. They even take them to school and share them with their friends.

» **Vegetable Sticks or Crudités** Dipped in houmous or one of my delicious spreads. The secret to making veggie sticks appetizing is in the chopping. Don't make the sticks too thick. Nice small, thin sticks are perfect. You can eat lots of them. Cucumbers, carrots, yellow and red peppers, celery make perfect veggie crudités.

ELEVEN
TREATS

You probably weren't expecting too many treats, but I love to create healthy alternatives to sugar-laden sweets and processed puds. I don't recommend eating these treats after dinner as they are best to digest earlier in the day. Sunday afternoons are my family's favourite time for a treat – the carob fudge brownies (p.217) are fantastic!

Chestnut cream parfait

SERVES 4

125 g dried chestnuts, presoaked for 12 hours or
overnight in cold water
50 g ground pecan pieces or almonds
250 ml rice milk
500 ml amasake
1 tsp vanilla essence
1 tsp ground cinnamon plus extra for garnish
quarter teaspoon ground nutmeg
2 tbsp agar agar flakes
1 tbsp almond flakes

1. Put the chestnuts in a medium-sized pan and cover
with 250 ml water. Bring to the boil, then lower the heat
and simmer for 20 minutes until tender. Drain and
reserve the cooking liquid.
2. Place the chestnuts in a food processor with the
pecans or almonds and blend until smooth. Add the rice
milk, amasake, vanilla, cinnamon and nutmeg and blend
until creamy.
3. Heat 125 ml of the reserved cooking liquid and add
the agar agar. Stir to dissolve and pour into the food
processor while it's running. Blend to combine well.
4. Pour into 4 serving glasses and chill until set.
Garnish with almond flakes and ground cinnamon.

Blueberry apple jelly

SERVES 4
1 litre freshly pressed apple juice
6 tbsp agar agar flakes
1 tsp natural vanilla essence
250 g fresh blueberries

1. Place the apple juice in a small saucepan and bring
to the boil. Add the agar agar flakes, then lower the heat
and simmer for 2 minutes.

2. Remove from the heat and allow to cool then add the
vanilla essence.

3. Place the blueberries in a glass bowl, pour over the
jelly and chill for 2 hours in the fridge to set.

Lemon pannacotta

I use the seaweed agar agar, which is a clear jelly-like liquid.
Because it tastes neutral, it can be used in sweet and savoury
recipes. It is cooling so can help the liver and other heat
conditions affecting the heart and lungs.

SERVES 4
500 ml rice milk
juice and zest of 1 lemon
1 tbsp barley malt syrup
2 dessertspoonfuls agar agar flakes

1. Bring the milk, lemon juice and barley malt syrup to
the boil. Lower the heat to a simmer and add the agar agar
and lemon zest. Cook for 3–4 minutes. Remove from the
heat and allow to cool.

2. Pour into 4 dariole (small cup-shaped) moulds and
chill for 2–3 hours until set.

Treats

Cinnamon rice pudding

This is a fantastic dessert that is loaded with B vitamins.
If you are stressed out, need to relax or just fancy something
that is naturally sweet, then this is the best dish going.

SERVES 4
325 g long grain brown rice
1.5 litres rice milk
1 cinnamon stick, broken in half
juice and zest of 1 lemon

1. Place the rice, rice milk, cinnamon and lemon juice
in a medium-sized pan. Bring to the boil, lower the heat
and simmer for 30–40 minutes, stirring occasionally. Add
a little more rice milk if required. The rice should be
very tender and the liquid well absorbed.
2. Serve hot or cold sprinkled with lemon zest.

Grilled banana with citrus spice

Researchers have found that three bananas contain
enough magnesium to quell a hayfever attack.

SERVES 4
4 bananas, peeled and sliced in half lengthways
juice of 1 lemon
2 tsp ground cinnamon
125 g fresh blueberries

1. Preheat the oven to 200C/gas mark 6.
2. Place the bananas on a baking tray, pour over
the lemon juice and sprinkle with the cinnamon.
3. Bake for 10–15 minutes until caramelized
4. Serve warm with fresh blueberries sprinkled on top.

Top tip

These fruit treats are delicious, but remember not to eat fruit as a dessert. For better digestion, enjoy these recipes a couple of hours before/after a meal.

Lemon mousse

More than half the people who come to see me test low in essential fatty acids (EFAs) – nutrients you need from your diet. Signs of EFA-deficiency can include dry, rough skin, skin problems, infertility, hair loss, dry hair, chapped lips and tiredness. This dessert is a fantastic source of those much-needed nutrients, mainly because of the avocados, which are high in EFAs. I often call essential fatty acids essential thinny acids to induce my clients to eat them. Please banish the fallacy that avocados are fattening. They are not. They are loaded with good fats, which play a vital role in weight management. I've combined the avocados here with fresh dates, which I think of as great anti-stressors. They're yummy too!

SERVES 4
4 whole lemons
4 ripe avocados, stoned, peeled and mashed
juice of half a lemon
juice of half an orange
250 g pitted dates
2 tbsp maple syrup
zest of 1 lemon

1. With a very sharp knife remove the skin from one of the lemons, leaving the body of the lemon whole. Cut in half and remove the seeds. Repeat for all the lemons.
2. Place all the ingredients, except the lemon zest, in a food processor and blend until smooth. Spoon into dessert dishes and chill for 2 hours in the fridge.
3. Serve garnished with lemon zest.

Treats

Pears in syrup

SERVES 4
4 pears, peeled
1 dessertspoon barley malt syrup
2 star anise

1. Place the pears in a pan large enough for them to fit snugly, add the syrup and star anise and cover in boiling water.
2. Bring back to the boil, then lower the heat and simmer for 10 minutes.
3. Allow pears to cool, then remove from the syrup.
4. Boil the syrup until it reduces to 100 ml.
5. Drizzle the thickened syrup over the pears and serve.

Baked apples with raisin compote

SERVES 4
4 cooking apples, cored and halved horizontally
2 tbsp raisins
2 tbsp sultanas
2 tbsp maple syrup

1. Preheat the oven to 200C/gas mark 6.
2. Place the apples in an ovenproof baking dish.
3. Mix the raisins and sultanas together and stuff them into the apple cores. Drizzle a little syrup into each apple.
4. Bake for 15–20 minutes and serve warm.

Treats

Lovers' passion fruit delight

SERVES 4
200 g fresh strawberries, hulled
4 passion fruit, halved
fresh mint leaves

1. Slice the strawberries and arrange in a fan shape
on a plate.
2. Scoop the passion fruit pulp on to the strawberries,
garnish with the mint leaves and serve.

Carob fudge brownie

MAKES 12 PIECES
WILL KEEP IN THE FRIDGE FOR UP TO 5 DAYS
300 g pitted dates
200 g soaked raisins
4 tbsp carob powder
500 g Brazil nuts, presoaked overnight in cold water
100 g ground flax seeds
100 g sunflower seeds
125 g chopped walnuts
125 g whole walnuts
sprinkle of sesame seeds

1. Place the dates, raisins, carob powder, Brazil nuts
and 500 ml water in a food processor and blend until you
have a smooth paste.
2. Mix through the seeds and walnuts.
3. Spread the mixture evenly on to a 10 x 20cm baking
tray lined with cling film. Sprinkle with sesame seeds
then freeze for 1 hour.
4. Cut into 12 pieces and serve.

TWELVE
STOCKS, SAUCES & DRESSINGS

Last but not least, try my homemade stocks, sauces and dressings. They can turn an everyday meal into a taste sensation. Most of them can be chilled or frozen and make a simple and delicious addition to many meals.

Quick salad dressing

Not many people know that ready-made mayonnaise can
be thinned down really easily with water to make a simple
dressing. This one is flavoured with fresh herbs, dill or mint
for example, but you could use dried herbs or even add finely
grated lemon rind for a zesty flavour.

MAKES 70 ML
2 tbsp Egg-Free Mayonnaise (see p.225)
2 tbsp chopped fresh herbs

Place the mayonnaise and the herbs in a small screw-top
jar along with 2 tablespoons of water, shake well and serve.
This dressing needs to be used on the day of making.

Herby salad dressing

MAKES 130 ML
KEEPS FOR THREE DAYS IN THE FRIDGE
8 tbsp olive oil
2 tbsp cider vinegar
1 tsp Dijon mustard
half a garlic clove, peeled and chopped
1 tbsp chopped fresh herbs
quarter teaspoon wheat-free vegetable bouillon powder

Place all the ingredients, together with 2 tablespoons
of cold water, in a small screw-top jar and shake well.

Sesame miso dressing

MAKES 130 ML
KEEPS FOR THREE DAYS IN THE FRIDGE
3 tbsp sesame oil
2 tbsp cider vinegar
2 tbsp light yellow miso
1 garlic clove, peeled and crushed
half a teaspoon chopped fresh basil
half a teaspoon chopped fresh oregano

Place all the ingredients, together with 6 tablespoons
of cold water, in a small screw-top jar and shake well.

Onion gravy

Never underestimate the power of onions. They can aid in
the lowering of blood pressure and cholesterol and can keep
colds at bay. And my onion gravy makes the Aduki Bean
Stew on page 157 taste out of this world.

MAKES 250 ML
KEEPS IN THE FRIDGE FOR THREE DAYS
2 onions, peeled and sliced
1 tsp olive oil
2 tsp tamari sauce
2 tsp arrowroot

1. Place the onions, olive oil and 6 tablespoons of water
in a medium-sized pan and cook gently for 15–20 minutes
until the onions are very soft.
2. Mix the tamari with the arrowroot and add to the
onion mixture, along with 500 ml water, mixing well.
3. Cook over a medium heat for 10 minutes and serve hot.

Stocks, sauces and dressings

221

Vegetable stock

MAKES 1 LITRE
KEEPS IN THE FRIDGE FOR FIVE DAYS OR
IN THE FREEZER FOR A MONTH

1 onion, peeled and sliced
2 leeks, washed, trimmed and sliced
1 fennel bulb, trimmed and sliced
2 carrots, trimmed, peeled and chopped
1 handful fresh parsley stalks
1 tsp coriander seeds
2 fresh bay leaves
2 sprigs fresh thyme

1. Place all the ingredients in a large casserole and pour in boiling water to cover.

2. Bring back to the boil, then lower the heat and simmer for 45 minutes.

3. Strain through a fine sieve and cover. Discard the vegetables.

Roasted vegetable stock

This veggie stock is a great alternative to stock cubes or
bouillon powder. Perfect for anyone on a low-salt diet, it's
full of rich, natural flavours that will add an amazing zest
to your stews and soups. It's also the ideal way to use up
a glut of root vegetables, so don't worry if you find yourself
throwing in different vegetables each time you make it.

Make this stock in large quantities to save time later.
Use it as a base for stews and soups. It is already diluted,
so there's no need to add any extra water. Just use the same
amount of stock as the amount of liquid called for in
the recipe.

For easier storage reduce the stock down to 250 ml
and store in ice trays in the freezer. Rehydrate 1 cube to
3 parts water.

MAKES 1 LITRE
**KEEPS FOR ONE WEEK IN THE FRIDGE OR ONE MONTH
IN THE FREEZER**
6 garlic cloves, unpeeled
3 carrots, trimmed, peeled and chopped
2 red onions, peeled and quartered
2 parsnips, trimmed, peeled and sliced
2 celery stalks, trimmed and chopped
1 sweet potato, peeled and chopped
1 leek, washed, trimmed and thickly sliced
2 sprigs fresh rosemary
1 fresh bay leaf

1. Preheat the oven to 200C/gas mark 6.
2. Place all the ingredients in a roasting pan and roast
for 40–45 minutes.
3. Remove the garlic and transfer the other ingredients
to a large saucepan. Cover with 1.25 litres water, bring
to the boil and squeeze the garlic into the stock. Reduce
heat and simmer the stock for 45 minutes.
4. Strain through a sieve and cool.

Stocks, sauces and dressings

223

Tangy barbecue relish

MAKES 425 ML
KEEPS FOR THREE DAYS IN THE FRIDGE
2 garlic cloves, peeled and finely chopped
1 red onion, peeled and finely sliced
400-g can chopped organic tomatoes
1 tbsp chopped fresh basil

1. Place all the ingredients except the basil in a small saucepan. Bring to the boil, then lower the heat and simmer, stirring occasionally, for 30–40 minutes, until the mixture is soft and syrupy. Add a little water if necessary during the cooking process.
2. Transfer into a small bowl, cover and chill. Serve with freshly chopped basil.

Egg-free mayonnaise

MAKES 325 ML
KEEPS FOR TWO DAYS IN THE FRIDGE
300 g drained tofu, roughly chopped
1 tbsp olive oil
juice of half a lemon
1 tbsp cider vinegar (or brown rice vinegar)
1 garlic clove, peeled and crushed

1. Place all the ingredients, together with 2 tablespoons
of cold water, in a food processor and blend until smooth.
2. Transfer to a small bowl, cover and chill.

Home-made tomato ketchup

Molasses adds an intriguing sweet flavour and plenty of
access to the all-important B vitamins that so many of us
are lacking, but you may well find the ketchup sweet enough
without it.

MAKES 300 ML
KEEPS FOR THREE DAYS IN THE FRIDGE
6 ripe tomatoes, quartered
1 red pepper, deseeded and chopped
1 small red onion, peeled and chopped
1 garlic clove, peeled and finely chopped
3 tbsp cider vinegar (or brown rice vinegar)
half a teaspoon molasses

1. Place all the ingredients in a medium-sized saucepan
and cook over a moderate heat for 40 minutes. Stir
occasionally and add a little extra water if required.
2. Remove from the heat and cool for a few minutes.
Blend in a food processor or with a hand-held blender.
Pass through a sieve and discard the seeds and pips.
3. Allow to cool then transfer to a bowl. Cover and chill
until required.

Flavoured oils

Here are three different-flavoured oils. Simply fill three
sterile bottles with olive oil and add the ingredients by using
a wooden skewer to push them under the oil. These oils will
keep for one month in a dark cupboard.

ORIENTAL
2 stalks lemon grass
6 fresh coriander stalks
2-cm piece fresh root ginger

MEDITERRANEAN
2 stalks fresh basil
2 sprigs fresh thyme
2 sprigs fresh oregano
6 garlic cloves, peeled

ROSEMARY
1 tsp coriander seeds
3–4 sprigs fresh rosemary

DR GILLIAN'S FINAL WORD

There's one last secret that you need
to know before I sign off. I want you
to start thinking about your body
as an energy system that absorbs
the positive energy of food and our
surrounding environment. Many
years ago, I used to eat out at a new
vegetarian restaurant that opened up
in my local neighbourhood. The first
time I ate there, the food was great and
I became a regular. When I went back
the following week, I noticed the food
tasted downright bad, and on certain
days I actually felt a lump in my throat
after eating there. Something wasn't
right and as it turned out, I learned
that the owner was in the kitchen in
a foul mood. She did not want to be
there. You could literally tell whether
she was there or not from the food.

Conversely, think about the mother
who lovingly serves up dinner to her
children, or whips up chicken soup
when they have a cold. The emotional

nourishment and warm healing is immense when the energy is right. So here are your two simple assignments:

First, always prepare your food with a sense of happiness, kindness, compassion, fun and love. Even if you don't feel so positive before preparing a meal, then take a few moments out to shift your mood.

Second, when you go shopping for your fruits and vegetables, take a minute to feel the energy of the produce as well as your own body's energies. Ask yourself what looks good? What looks healthy? What's screaming out at me? What do I feel like eating today? In this way, you will begin to raise your level of energy consciousness in relation to foods and the body's delicate balance.

Allow this energetic sensitivity to guide your choices of ingredients and how you prepare and serve a meal. This is my greatest discovery for wellness. Until next time . . .

Dr Gillian's final word

ACKNOWLEDGEMENTS

This cookbook is dedicated to my two dearest wee lassies
who have even gone so far as to sample all of the seaweeds
that I advocate and who also put up with my long weekend
hours and shifts late into the night writing this book.
To Howard for the most incredible inspiration to share
information, for your motivation, words and help,
monumental appreciation and gratitude. Words don't
do justice to the enormity of your contribution. By the
way, you make the most incredible quinoa porridge.

Nicola: You are an extraordinary woman with great
vision. You and your team have all been incredible, working
so hard every single day: Julia, Jo, Jina, Dawn and Helen.
To Luigi, whose skills still seem to be out of this world.
Thanks to Kate Adams, Chantal Gibbs, Louise Moore,
Tom Weldon and the team at Penguin – this book could
not exist without you; to Smith & Gilmour for incredible
design and Helen Tillott for your creativity.

Words are never going to be enough to express the
dedication and diligence from all involved at McKeith
Research Ltd, especially Alan, Indranie and Robert.
And thanks to Theresa for your fantastic, cutting-
edge research.

Much appreciation must go to ZH, who claims she
hardly ever cooked in her own house until I had her
experiment with many of my recipes. Thanks for keeping
things together throughout this project. A big thank-you
to Izabela and thanks to Oscar, who always gets me from
point A to B on time, even when I am not. What would
I do without you? Oscar has taught me that we get
wiser as we get older.

To my rocks Doug and Eloise Nelson: much love and gratitude always.

Thanks to Josie, Mandy and Paula.

And what would I do without Justine for your unwavering support, creativity, and help with food and styling. Much love and hugs. Thanks too to Gileng, Mari and Angie. Appreciation to Montse Bradford of the Natural Cookery School.

Thanks to everyone at Channel Four: for the platform to share this information.

Huge hugs and thanks to my TV participants for doing everything I say and feeling so well. You have transformed your lives and in the process are transforming the nation.

Deep gratitude to Lucy, Louise and Max for getting the word out. You're all fantastic. And also to Yvette and Melissa for your incredible support and warmth throughout.

Much love to Mum and Dad for always believing in me.

Thanks to Chaim Solomon for his spiritual guidance.

INDEX

Live more